AF617923

Tumbling Ruins

DISTANZ

Tumbling Ruins

Henrike Naumann
with Angela Schönberger
and Andreas Brandolini

KONTEXT

Contents

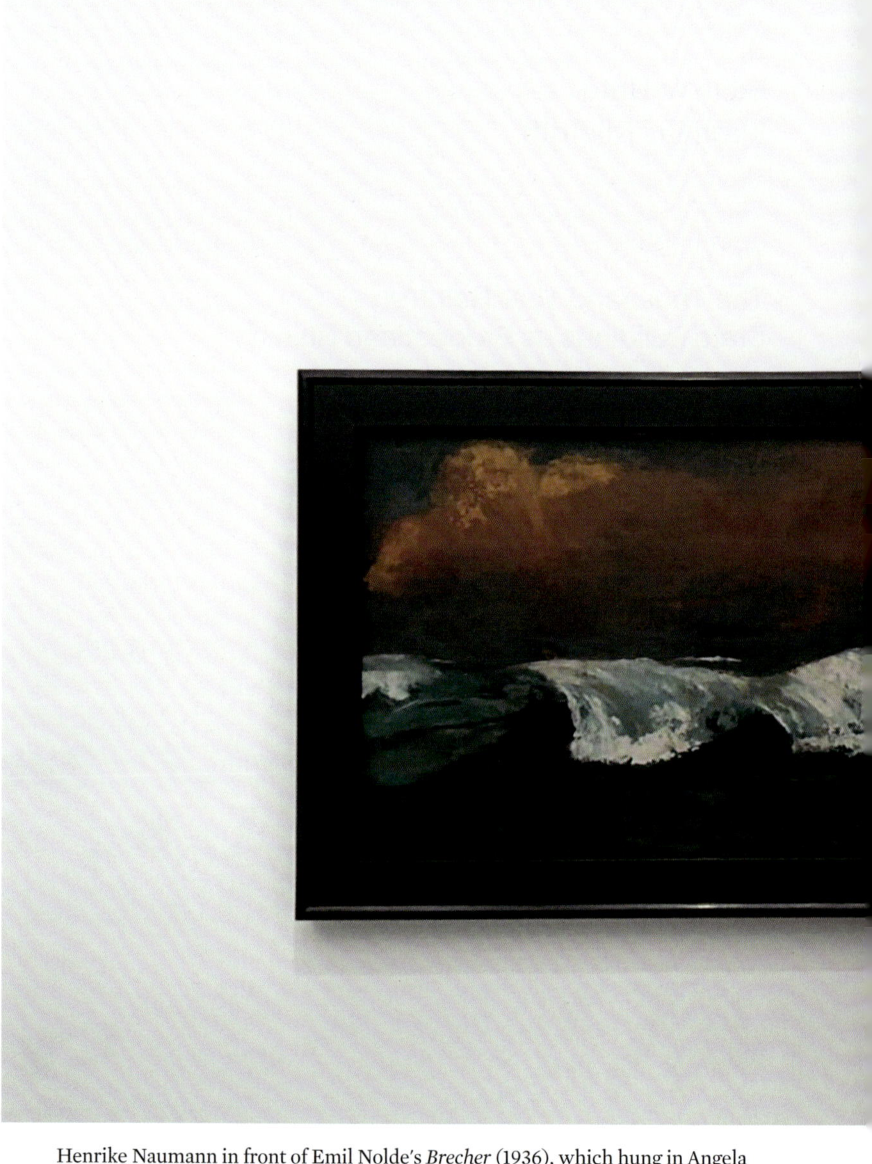

Henrike Naumann in front of Emil Nolde's *Brecher* (1936), which hung in Angela Merkel's office at the Federal Chancellery (2006–2019). The photo was taken in 2019 at the exhibition *Emil Nolde—A German Legend: The Artist under National Socialism* at the Hamburger Bahnhof in Berlin. The exhibition explored Nolde's relation to National Socialism. After the exhibition, the wall in Merkel's office remained empty.

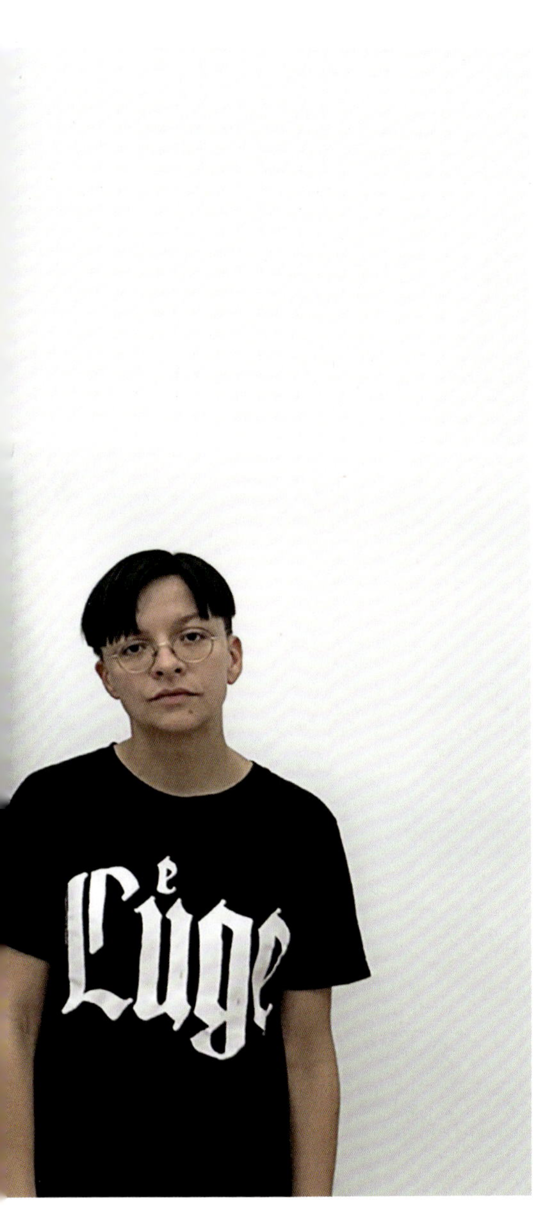
Lüge

Editor's Note

Matthias Kliefoth

I first encountered Henrike Naumann's art in her deeply moving exhibition *DDR NOIR: Schichtwechsel* (2018), which prompted some searching reflections—on my own past as well as the future. A native of Zwickau, then in East Germany, the artist makes installations that uncover historical facts and their lingering impact on the present. Sampling furniture, everyday implements, and design artifacts she finds or purchases on eBay Kleinanzeigen,[1] she discusses the histories of the objects that surround us and fashions rooms inhabited by the collective memory of residential life. Not concerned with beauty or the fetishism of high-quality design, she unfolds an archaeology of fascism in Germany, the country's partition during the cold war, its reunification, and other toxic issues—an undertaking that scrutinizes "German identity" through the lens of its own four walls and reminds all of us of our shared responsibility.

We cannot escape our history. Our lifestyles and consumer goods are saturated with it. Naumann uses design to interrogate these social structures: in this book, a 1990s wall unit transforms into the Alpine panorama that Adolf Hitler overlooked from his mountainside villa. Veneered plywood meets a spruce

1. eBay Kleinanzeigen is an online second hand sales plattform in Germany.

forest. Flokati seat cushions, carried by mannequins sold in drawing supplies stores, mimic the festive procession presenting a model of the House of German Art in Munich (today's Haus der Kunst)—one of the Nazi regime's earliest monumental edifices, to be built after designs by Paul Ludwig Troost.

Angela Schönberger wrote her dissertation in the 1970s on the New Reich Chancellery building as a central scene of Nazi crimes and on Albert Speer's theory of ruin value. Her essay, first published in its present form in 1987, analyzes how National Socialism, under a cover of opaque architectural theorizing, took built form—until its own implosion and the ruination of its legacy.

Andreas Brandolini was a cofounder of the avant-garde New German Design movement of the 1980s. His *German Living Room* at documenta 8 (1987) has been hailed as seminal, signaling a break with the stifling dogmatism of the industrial design of the time. Taking a laconic view of the dictum of "good form," he and Naumann discuss the potential of anti-icons.

When social, political, and cultural debates touch on the alleged danger of a loss of culture and identity, our visceral reaction is to man the barricades. The battle lines are drawn, reconciliation seems inconceivable: think of the storming of the U.S.

Capitol on January 6, 2021, of the assailants' Viking masks and their boasting of their exploits with trophy pictures posted on social media. History repeats itself. Right-wing movements are agile and aggressive, cloaking themselves in esoteric beliefs, shamanism, and folklore. Tomorrow's trends are being born today, behind the closed doors of our living rooms. Our things could tell us a great deal, if we would listen.

The Thousand-Year Reich's State Buildings as Predestined Ruins?

Angela Schönberger

On Albert Speer's theory of ruin value.[1]

Since the publication of Albert Speer's memoirs, *Inside the Third Reich,* in 1969, his therein presented "A Theory of Ruin Value" of the buildings representative of "Third Reich" has attracted particular attention in specialist literature. It seemed to offer surprising new insights into his building philosophy and into a preference for natural stone that could almost be interpreted iconologically and which largely determined the appearance of National Socialist power architecture.

In 1935, Albert Speer, Hitler's architect and general building inspector for the "Greater Germanic Reich" and later armaments minister, had seen the blasted reinforced concrete structure of a building on his way to the construction site of the Nazi Party Rally Grounds in Nuremberg. The demolished and desolate sight inspired him to the following reflections: "... buildings of modern construction," Speer wrote in his memoirs *Inside the Third Reich,* "were poorly suited to form that 'bridge of tradition' to future generations which Hitler was calling for. It was hard to imagine that rusting heaps of rubble could communicate these heroic inspirations which Hitler admired in the monuments of the past.

1. This essay first appeared in: *IDEA. Werke, Theorien, Dokumente, Jahrbuch der Hamburger Kunsthalle VI,* 1987, edited by Werner Hoffmann and Martin Warnke.

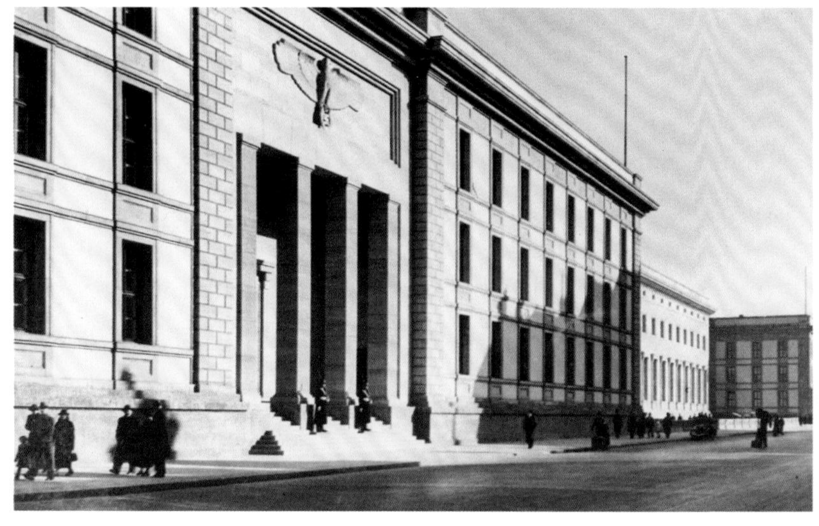

Fig. 1: Albert Speer, extension to the New Reich Chancellery in Berlin, façade on Voßstraße, 1939

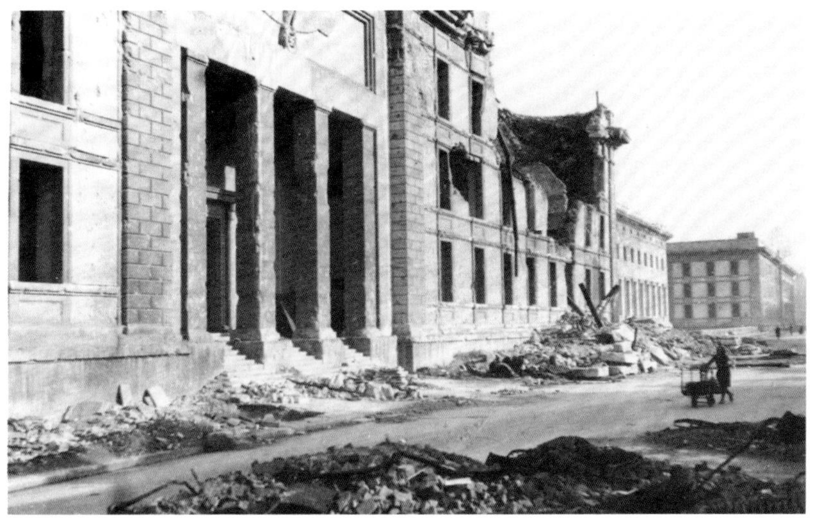

Fig. 2: Ruins of the New Reich Chancellery, façade on Voßstraße, 1946

My 'theory' was intended to deal with this dilemma. By using special materials and by applying certain principles of statics, we should be able to build structures which even in a state of decay, after hundreds or (such were our reckonings) thousands of years would more or less resemble Roman models."[2]

To illustrate his thoughts, he then had a drawing made: "It showed what the reviewing stand on the Zeppelin Field would look like after generations of neglect, overgrown with ivy, its columns fallen, the walls crumbling here and there, but the outlines still clearly recognizable."[3]

It may come as a surprise that the architect Albert Speer—while he was busy with the plans for the vast party conference site in Nuremberg (fig. 3), with important designs for the new building of the Reich Chancellery in Berlin (fig. 1), and presumably already with preliminary considerations for the gigantic undertaking of redesigning Berlin into the "Germania" capital for a Greater Germanic Empire—while he was occupied with all these designs and preparing their realization, was already thinking of the state of decay, of the end of such still future architectures. The desire of an architect that his buildings should be documents of the history of his time and bear witness to it and also to himself long beyond his time, would be and is understandable. But

2. Albert Speer, *Inside the Third Reich,* New York 1969, p. 56.
3. Ibid.

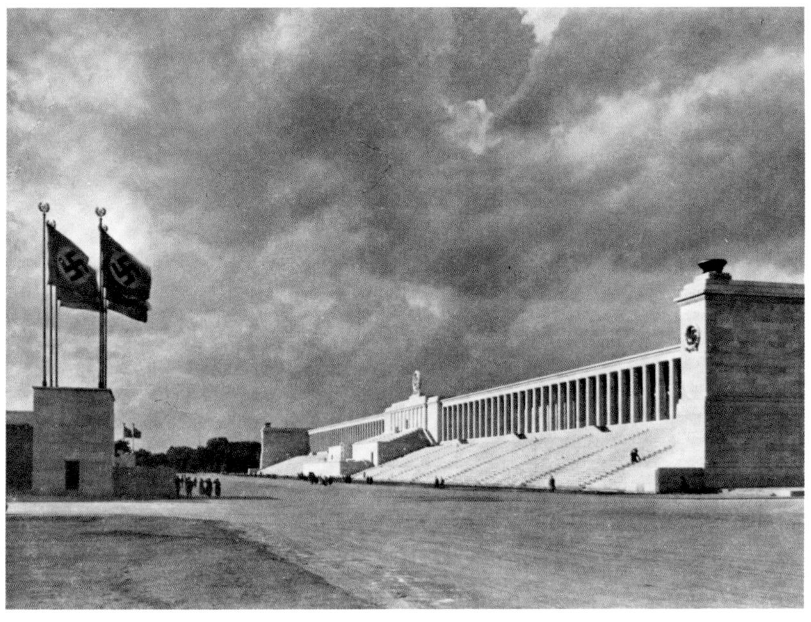

Fig. 3: Albert Speer, Zeppelin Field grandstand in Nuremberg, 1938

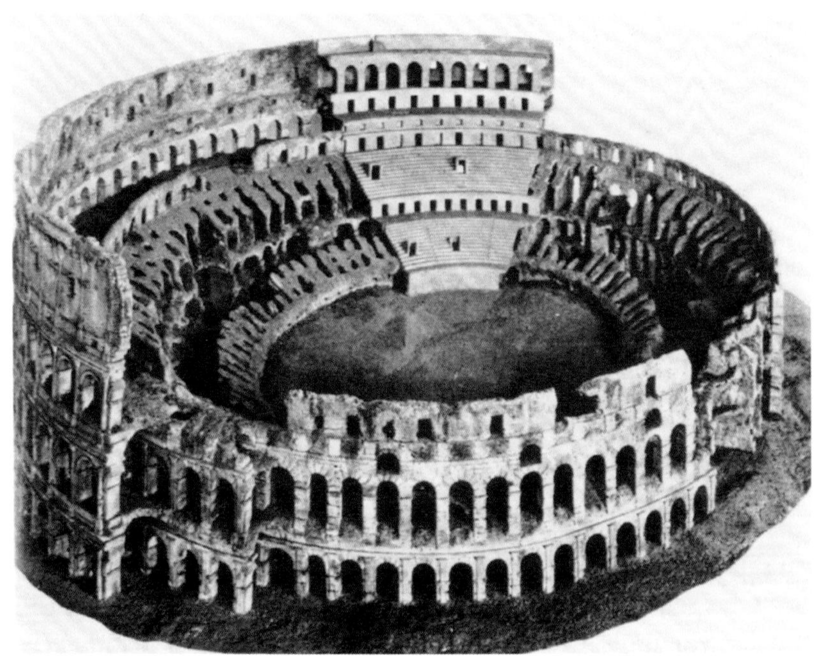

Fig. 4: Antonio Chichi, Amphitheatrum Flavium (Colosseum), Rome, cork model

Speer obviously wanted more. As a visionary, he saw in the power architectures of the "Third Reich," in his own buildings, authentic witnesses of present history for future generations that would exist in "thousands of years." Even as ruins, their grandeur should testify to the glory of their era. With such considerations, the claim to the timeless validity of these architectures, beyond material transience in the eyes of world history, would have been granted at the planning and execution stages.

According to Speer's description, his sketch seems to have reproduced an "orderly" architecture of ruins, not a field of rubble, not chaos. His description of the drawing spontaneously calls to mind the models of ancient ruins that were fashionable during the Classicist period, in which the material cork conveyed decay in aesthetic composition and descriptiveness (fig. 4).[4] Speer must have been familiar with such models due to his preoccupation with Classicist architecture. The overgrowth of ivy on the ruins mentioned by him was understood as an element from the spirit of Romanticism.

The idea of clear, one would almost like to say, clean conditions in decay seems to have played a decisive role in his considerations. The thought that ruins could also arise through abrupt destruction and then offer a sight of desolation has obviously been repressed.

4. Anita Büttner, *Korkmodelle von Antonio Chichi*. Offprint from: *Kunst in Hessen und am Mittelrhein*, no. 9 (supplement 1969).

Such a displacement could be based on Speer's aestheticism, which distanced itself from the actual events. This is proven by an almost unmasking quotation from his memoir *Inside the Third Reich,* when he writes about the events of *Kristallnacht* that "what really disturbed me at the time was the aspect of disorder ... charred beams, collapsed façades, burned-out walls—anticipations of a scene that during the war would dominate much of Europe. ... The smashed panes of shop windows offended my sense of middle-class order."[5] Revealed here are mechanisms of repression that point beyond such an individual statement and show the characteristically schizophrenic behavior of the "Third Reich" society, especially of its leaders in the face of a reality of horror, of brutal destruction. The inhuman works of the authorities' extermination were carried out in pedantic order according to bureaucratic planning. The "middle-class order" was not disturbed by them.

The drawing mentioned by Speer has not been preserved. Did it exist at all? Did Speer really have a vision of future ruins upon seeing that blown-up reinforced concrete structure and from it, as an architect, develop his mandate in the face of history to postpone the transience of his buildings into the distant future through the "special materials and by applying certain principles of statics" but even then, to let them at least appear in the form of "beautiful" ruins, as witnesses to historical greatness and his ingenuity?

5. See note 2, p. 111.

According to his memoirs *Inside the Third Reich,* Speer brought "A Theory of Ruin Value" to Hitler's attention and found understanding for these considerations from him, while those around him rejected them as downright blasphemous. "That I could even conceive of a period of decline for the newly founded Reich," Speer writes, "destined to last a thousand years seemed outrageous to many of Hitler's closest followers. But he himself accepted my ideas as logical and illuminating. He gave orders that, in the future, the important buildings of his Reich were to be erected in keeping with the principles of this 'law of ruins.'"[6] As the short-lived history of the "Third Reich" architecture and the contemporary documents prove, Hitler and Speer had natural stone in mind when it came to "special materials." Natural stone was now being trumpeted as a preeminent building material, the new discovery, as it were, for prestigious building under National Socialism. "When peoples inwardly experience great times," Hitler declared "they also give these times external expression. Their word is then more convincing than when it is spoken: it is the word in stone!"[7]

Behind the promotion of natural stone as the true "German" building material in contrast to the contemporary modern technologies and the materials

6. See note 2, p. 69.

7. Adolf Hitler: "Speech at the opening of the First German Architecture and Arts and Crafts Exhibition in Munich at the House of German Art on January 22, 1938," quoted from M. Domarus, *Hitler, Reden und Proklamationen 1932–1945,* vol. 1, Wiesbaden 1973.

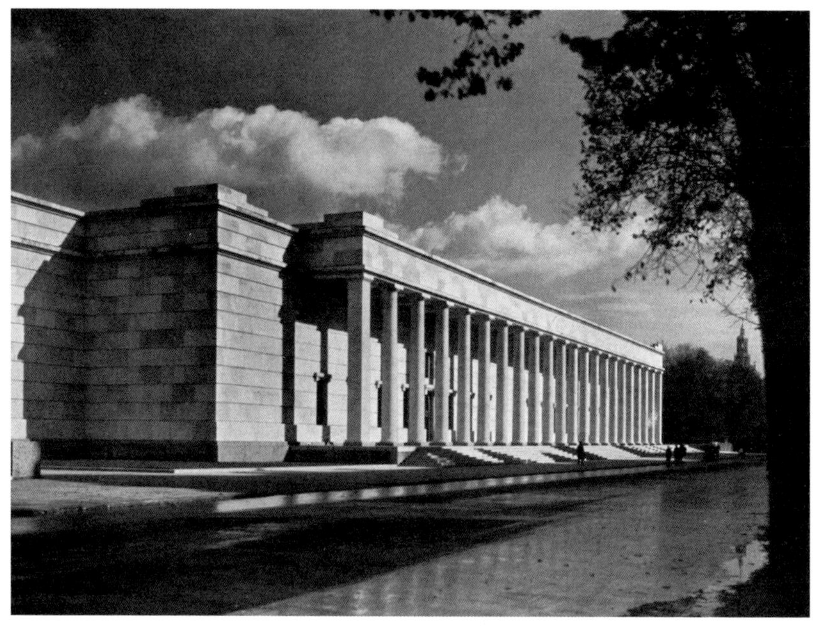

Fig. 5: Paul Ludwig Troost, House of German Art, Munich, 1938

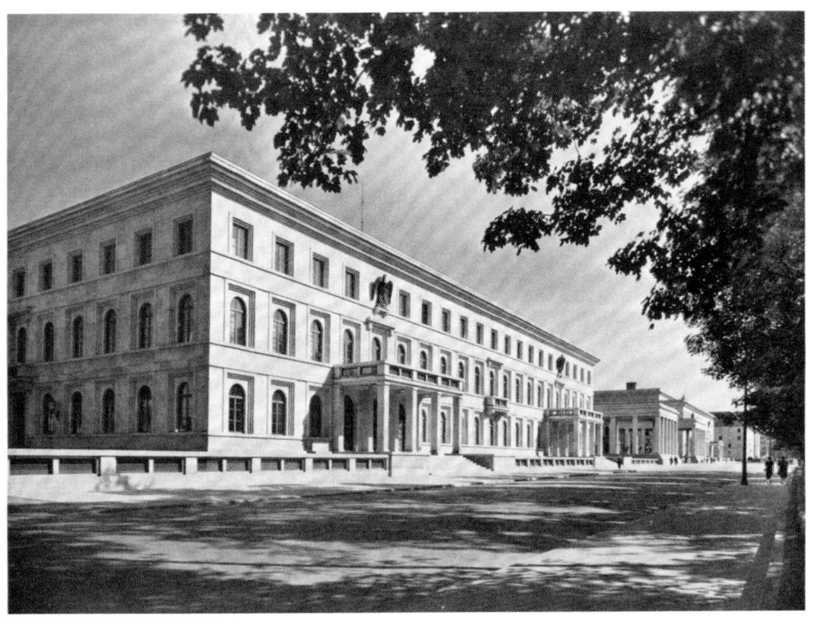

Fig. 6: Paul Ludwig Troost, NSDAP Fuhrer and Administration Building at Königsplatz in Munich, 1938

used—steel, concrete, and glass—was the intention to stand out against the “international style” and the “building Bolshevism” of the Weimar Republic, to highlight their “characteristic” building as a new and outstanding “national” achievement. Now, natural stone, due to its preciousness, had always been considered suitable for emphasizing the representative character of buildings, such as in Wilhelminian architecture. Examples include the Leipzig Monument to the Battle of the Nations by Bruno Schmitz (1898–1913), the Berlin Reichstag building by Paul Wallot (1884–94), and Peter Behrens' Imperial Embassy in St. Petersburg (1911/12). In the 1920s, too, natural stone was valued as an expression of purely aesthetic quality and was placed as a smooth skin around the construction of a steel skeleton, as exemplified by Emil Fahrenkamp's Shell House in Berlin (1930/32), among others.

With the beginning of the “Third Reich,” architects strive to give their buildings the impression of durability and strength by using natural stone. The pretense is to use it not as a dazzling material but as a seemingly massive self-supporting structure. In fact, the early representative buildings of the “Third Reich” are still absolutely erected as modern steel skeleton buildings with natural stone cladding: E.g. the House of German Art (1937, fig. 5), the two Führer buildings on Königsplatz in Munich (1937, fig. 6) by Paul Ludwig Troost; also the grandstand of the Zeppelin Field (fig. 3) in Nuremberg and even the German Pavilion at the World's Fair in Paris (1937, fig. 7) by Albert Speer.

Due to their increasingly rich architectural structure, however, they appear visually as purely natural stone buildings. A supportive compact brick masonry, which simulates a solid construction, is concealed behind the façade of Speer's New Reich Chancellery (1939, fig. 1) Steel was used here only for large spans, foundations, and roof structures.[8]

Should Speer's "A Theory of Ruin Value" be applied here, or had there been other reasons for the massive construction method and use of natural stone in the state buildings of the "Third Reich"?

1936 saw the beginning of a new intensive phase of war preparations. Towards the end of the year, Hitler announced the Four-Year Plan, which was intended to help overcome the problematic raw materials and foreign exchange situation in order to ensure the rapid realization of plans for conquest. However, the most essential raw material and import commodity for the armaments industry was iron ore, which became a crucial building material in the construction industry as structural steel. The Four-Year Plan, therefore, contained laws that were particularly relevant to the construction industry. Thus, as of December 1, 1936, all "private and public building and civil engineering projects" had to be reported before construction began. Such control

8. For general information on the architectural history of the Neue Reichskanzlei, see Angela Schönberger, *Die Neue Reichskanzlei von Albert Speer. Zum Zusammenhang von nationalsozialistischer Ideologie und Architektur*, Berlin 1981.

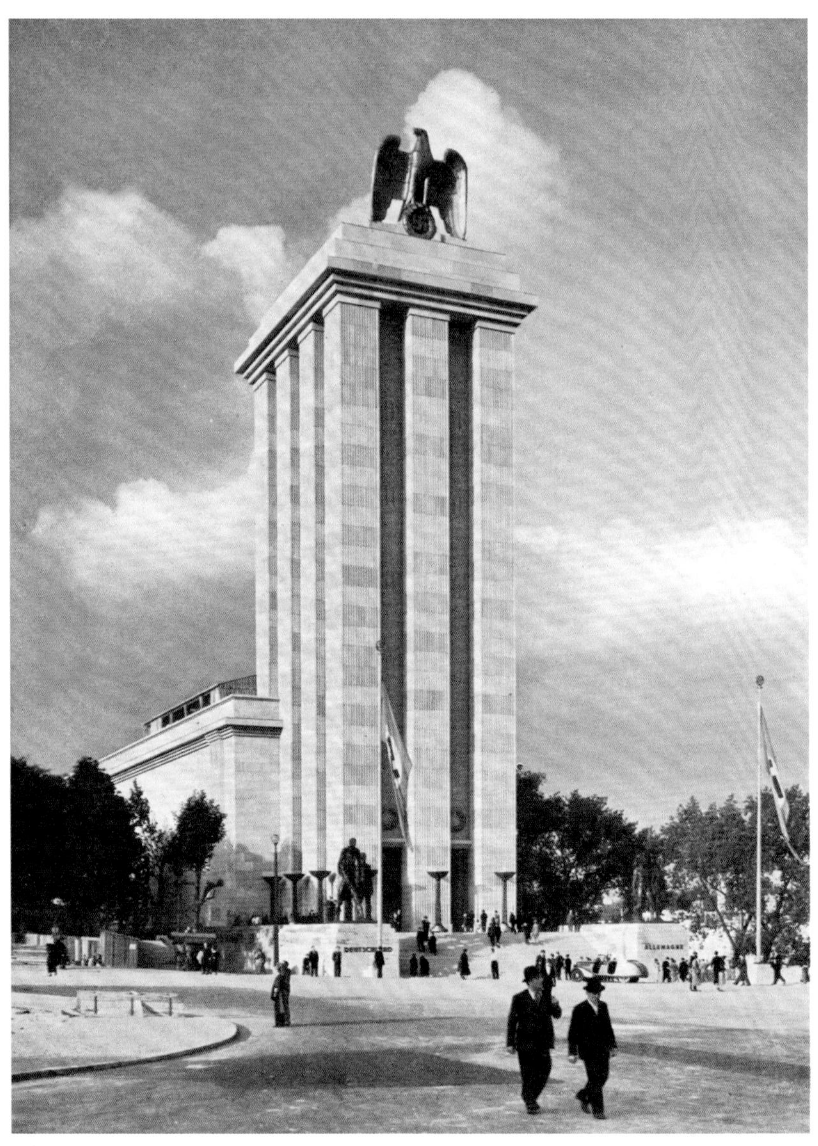

Fig. 7: Albert Speer, German Pavilion at the World's Fair in Paris, 1937

made it possible to direct the demand for building materials and labor and meet the war economy's demands. Finally, in 1939, the office of "General Plenipotentiary for the Regulation of the Construction Industry" was created, which Fritz Todt took over as "Inspector General for German Roadways." Building materials and construction workers were distributed to nineteen "contingent carriers," the most important of which was the Wehrmacht High Command.[9]

This legal regulation of the consumption of raw materials was intended both to secure the iron requirements for the armaments industry and to guarantee the necessary "demand for building materials for the execution of construction projects of national political significance within the framework of the Four-Year Plan." This meant industrial plants such as the Hermann-Göring-Werke in the vicinity of today's Salzgitter, military buildings, and fortifications such as the construction of the Westwall. However, despite the switch to massive construction, sufficient quantities of steel also had to be reserved for the planned state buildings. The Great Hall in Berlin (fig. 8), for example, was to be vaulted by a double-shell dome of steel and concrete construction with a width of 250-meters. The representative buildings on the Great Square and the North-South Axis, with their pompous staircases and huge halls, could not have been realized without steel

9. From 1937 onward, the decrees and laws were published continuously in the journal *Der Vierjahresplan, Zeitschrift für nationalsozialistische Wirtschaftspolitik*.

structures. Nevertheless, they were planned as far as possible using mixed construction with stone cladding.

"Stone instead of iron" was the motto of Albert Speer's recommendation in January 1937: "The successful implementation of the Four-Year Plan requires the cooperation of the architect in a very particular way. He must help in the task of eliminating, as far as possible, all building materials whose raw materials we must obtain from abroad and use for the time being for more urgent purposes. Presently, for building construction it is above all a building material whose consumption seems to be a natural necessity with each building, iron! ... In the west and south of Germany, where inexhaustible quantities of natural stone are everywhere in the landscape, there is an opportunity to use this most beautiful natural building material in the most abundant measure." When comparing the building materials of iron and stone, Speer cited lack of experience and uncertainty associated with steel frame construction as reasons for stone construction. "In no way, however, has it yet been possible to form the new building materials in such a way that they would be anywhere near the durability of stone construction and, in some respects, of wood. While only a few permanently strained iron bridge structures or halls have survived more than fifty years, the stone buildings of the Egyptians and Romans, which are thousands of years old, still stand today as tremendous building witnesses of great people's pasts."

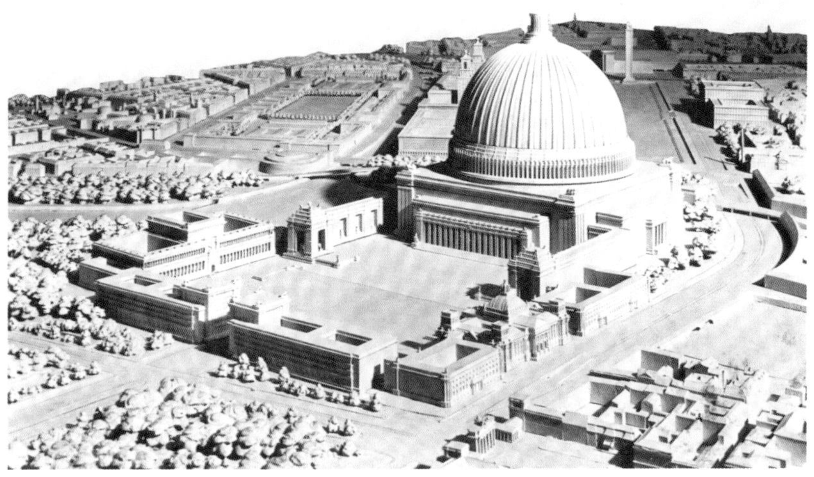

Fig. 8: Albert Speer, Model of the Great Hall in Berlin

Two illustrations (figs. 9, 10) of the Parthenon and a scaffolded steel skeleton structure illustrate the text as positive and negative examples. It goes on to say: "In all cases where it is possible, preference should be given to stone over the materials of iron and concrete, which have not yet been tested over long periods." The article ends with an appeal to the architect: "He should choose the stone which offers him all formal possibilities and which alone, through its durability, offers the future the tradition which for us today lies in the stone buildings of our past."[10]

In the same year, the building industry was called upon by the "Office for Resources and Materials" to pursue every justifiable possibility of economizing iron by making suitable changes to their building methods and designs, i.e., "by avoiding highly iron-consuming architectural additions in the form of deep projecting oriels, gables, towers, cupolas, a concentration of balconies, etc., to keep the proportion of building iron required from the iron quota of the Four-Year Plan as small as possible."[11]

This explains, among other things, why the housing estates in the "Third Reich" often look monotonous and barracks-like, with small windows and only rarely balconies. Housing construction, to the extent that there could be any question of it at all, had already been so curtailed in its construction material requirements

10. Albert Speer: "Stein statt Eisen," in: *Der Vierjahresplan 1,* 1937, pp. 135ff.
11. "Roh- und Werkstoffwirtschaft," in: *Der Vierjahresplan 1,* 1937, p. 345.

and limited to the most necessary that further cutbacks were no longer possible. Only industrial high-rises, public buildings, and road construction and civil engineering, which accounted for "30 % of the construction industry's estimated 35 % share of German crude iron demand," would have been considered for cuts in construction iron.

However, the construction of buildings in natural stone or at least with natural stone cladding meant the use of expensive materials, more labor time, and thus higher construction costs, making it largely unsuitable for the private sector. In fact, by 1938, 80 % and 1939, 100 % of the construction volume in Germany was financed exclusively by the public sector. "In practical terms, therefore, the transition to purely massive construction from natural or other stone only comes into question for those construction projects in which economic efficiency does not play such a major role. This applies in particular to representative buildings, both for the public sector and for industry, whose construction costs are measured according to different standards than, for instance, the construction costs for erecting an industrial plant."[12]

The sums calculated for just one building complex are illustrated by the planned Army High Command and the Soldiers' Hall by Wilhelm Kreis in Berlin. By the end of the war, work had been carried out using

12. Alfred Müller: "Die bauwirtschaftlichen Aufgaben der Industrie der Steine und Erden," in: *Der Vierjahresplan* 2, 1938, pp. 333ff.

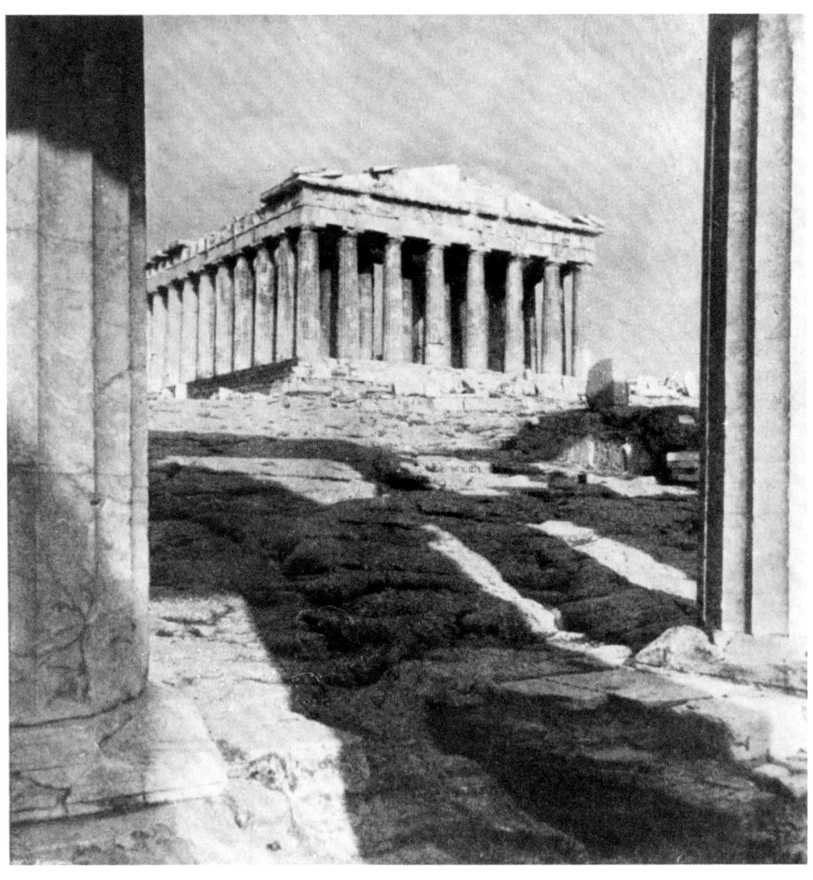

Fig. 9: "The Parthenon. The stone buildings of antiquity, in their present state, show the durability of the natural building material."—Albert Speer

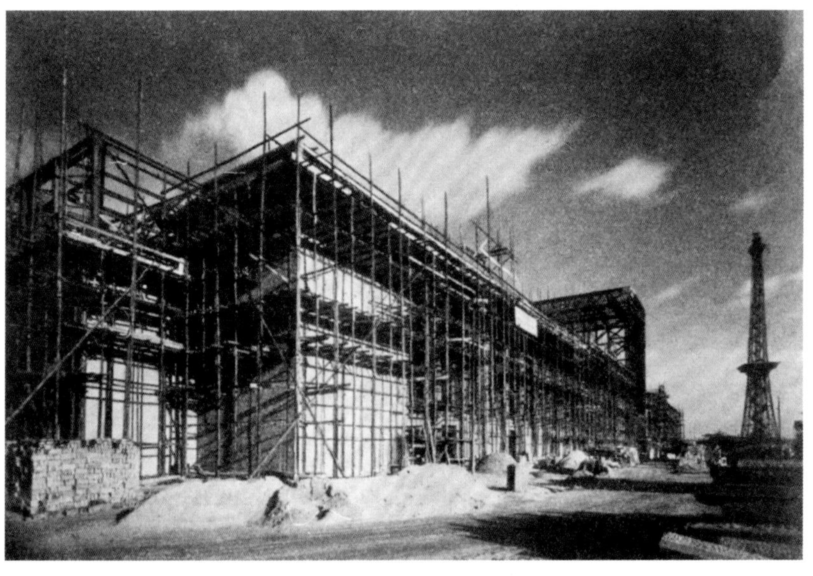

Fig. 10: “In iron frame construction, the supporting iron skeleton is clad in stone, simulating a solid building. The durability of such structures has not yet been tested in any way at present.”—Albert Speer

construction stone to the value of RM 21 million, and sixty-two companies had been contracted for these stone deliveries alone.[13] However, this is only a fraction of the amount of stone material that would have been used for the North-South Axis and the planned buildings on the Great Square in Berlin. During 1941, Speer, as General Inspector for the redesign of Berlin, who maintained a "Stone Commission" within his authority, awarded supply contracts totaling RM 30 million to Sweden, Norway, Finland, Italy, Belgium, and Holland. In addition, framework contracts for ten-year supply agreements were concluded with Sweden and Norway.[14] It should be remembered that these countries, except Italy and Sweden, were occupied by Germany. Norwegian granite was shipped to Holland and processed there. Speer had a cargo fleet established, which included up to 1,000 barges, for the transportation of the construction stone to Berlin. Moreover, the Sachsenhausen, Buchenwald, Mauthausen, and Flossenbürg concentration camps were used to process the building stone. In general, the architectural redesign of Berlin was to be carried out primarily with cheap labor such as forced laborers, prisoners of war, and concentration camp inmates. Authorities and industry bargained for forced laborers like a commodity or shifted them as favors. For example, in 1941, Heydrich promised Speer the transfer

13. *Oberfinanzdirektion Berlin, Akten der Sondervermögens- und Bauverwaltung, Übersicht über das Vermögen des früheren Generalinspektors für die Reichshauptstadt,* August 16, 1945, p. 8.

14. BA Koblenz R3/1735, *Chronik des Generalinspektors für die Reichshauptstadt 1941*, p. 77.

of 15,000 Czech workers in exchange for architectural advice and assistance. Furthermore, it was agreed between the two "that the Protectorate will provide annually 50,000 Czechs of the younger age groups for the purposes of the Berlin post-war duties, with a longer work obligation." Such an effort makes it strikingly clear that in the case of "representative buildings, economic efficiency does not play such a great role,"[15] For example, as the "Steine und Erden" (Stone and Earth) construction company, which collected large profits from the state contracts, stated at the time.

After all of the aspects mentioned above, the question arises as to whether Speer's "Theory of Ruin Value" determined the actual construction process or whether economic and power-political conditions rather decisively influenced the aesthetic design of representative architecture and housing construction.

In his memoirs, *Inside the Third Reich,* Speer had already called for the use of natural stone in 1935, i.e. one year before the Four-Year Plan came into force, and allegedly justified it to Hitler based on his "Theory of Ruin Value." It can be assumed with great certainty that he was aware of the Reich's economic difficulties due to war preparations at that time. Official propaganda rejected the use of reinforced concrete for state buildings for ideological reasons, while in reality, it was backed by the development of the armaments industry. Speer found a more subtle justification for the seemingly constructive use of natural stone in his

15. See note 13, p. 73.

"Theory of Ruin Value." However, there is no contemporary testimony for this theory. One must ask oneself whether Speer actually conceived it in 1935 or whether it was actually introduced into the memoirs by him only later as a subsequent fabrication and as evidence of his actual, purely artistic, architectural mindset.

Especially from today's retrospective view of the era of the "Third Reich," it seems like a historical irony that the state buildings erected for an eternity, insofar as the consequences of the war events destroyed them, did not differ in any way from the chaotic fields of rubble in the residential areas after only a few years (figs. 2, 11).

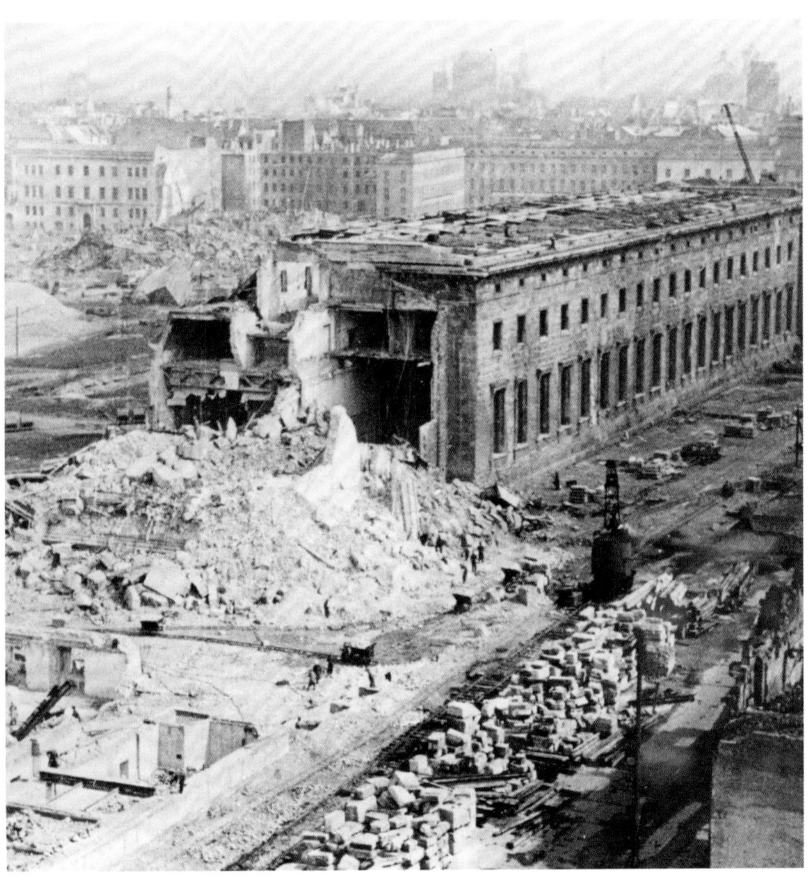

Fig. 11: Ruin of the New Reich Chancellery, 1949

Ruinenwert: A Research in Pictures

Henrike Naumann

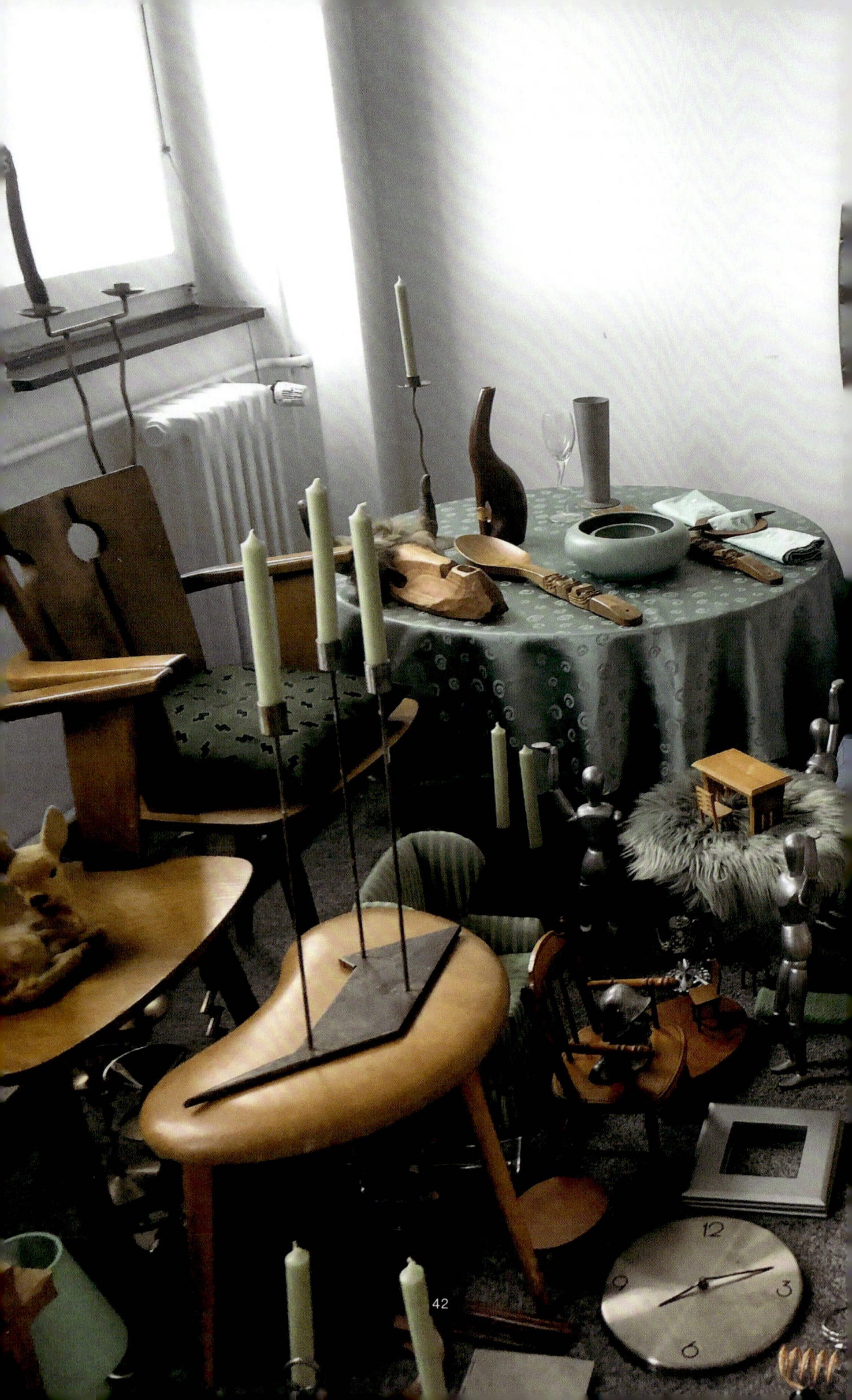
12
3
6
9

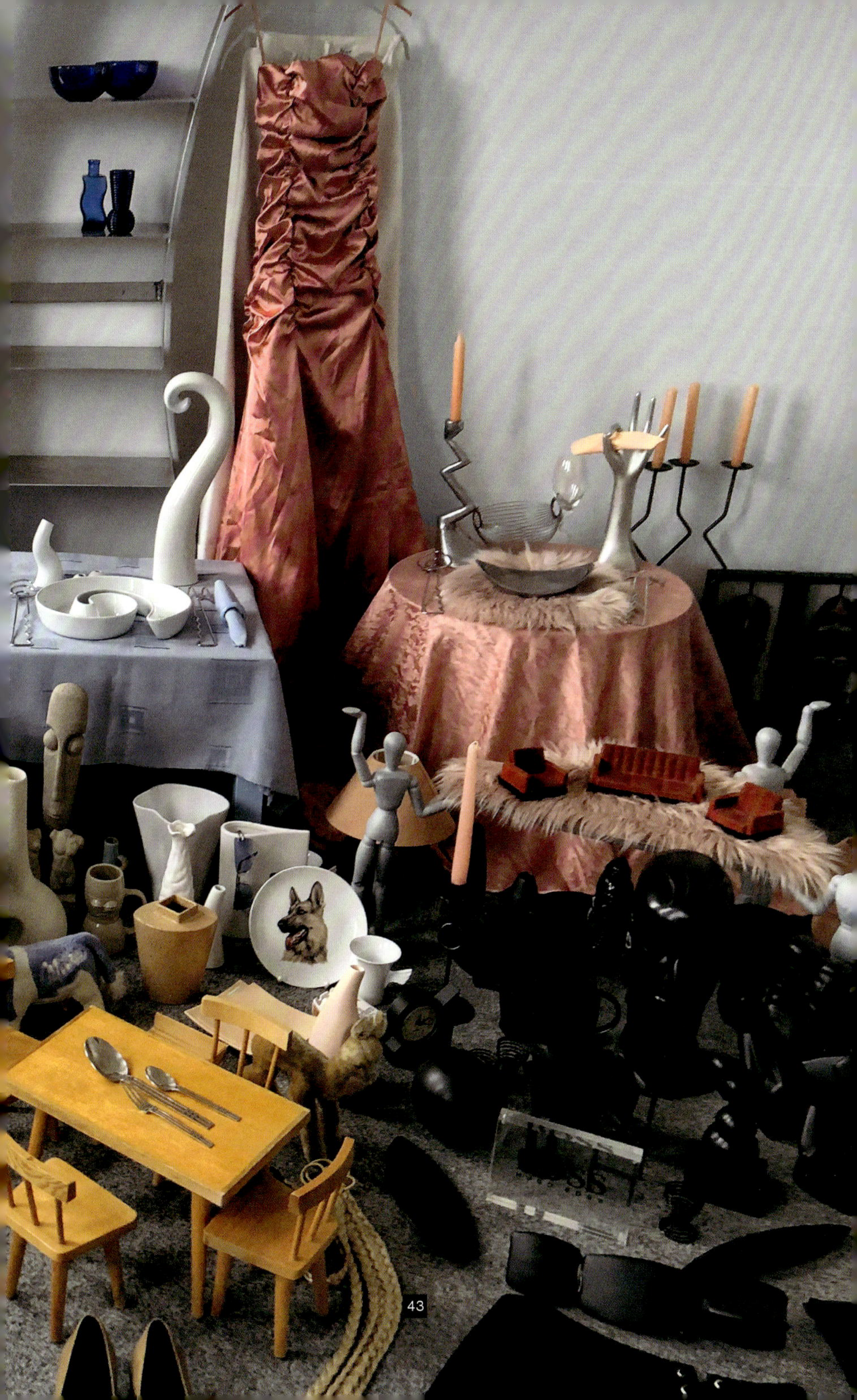

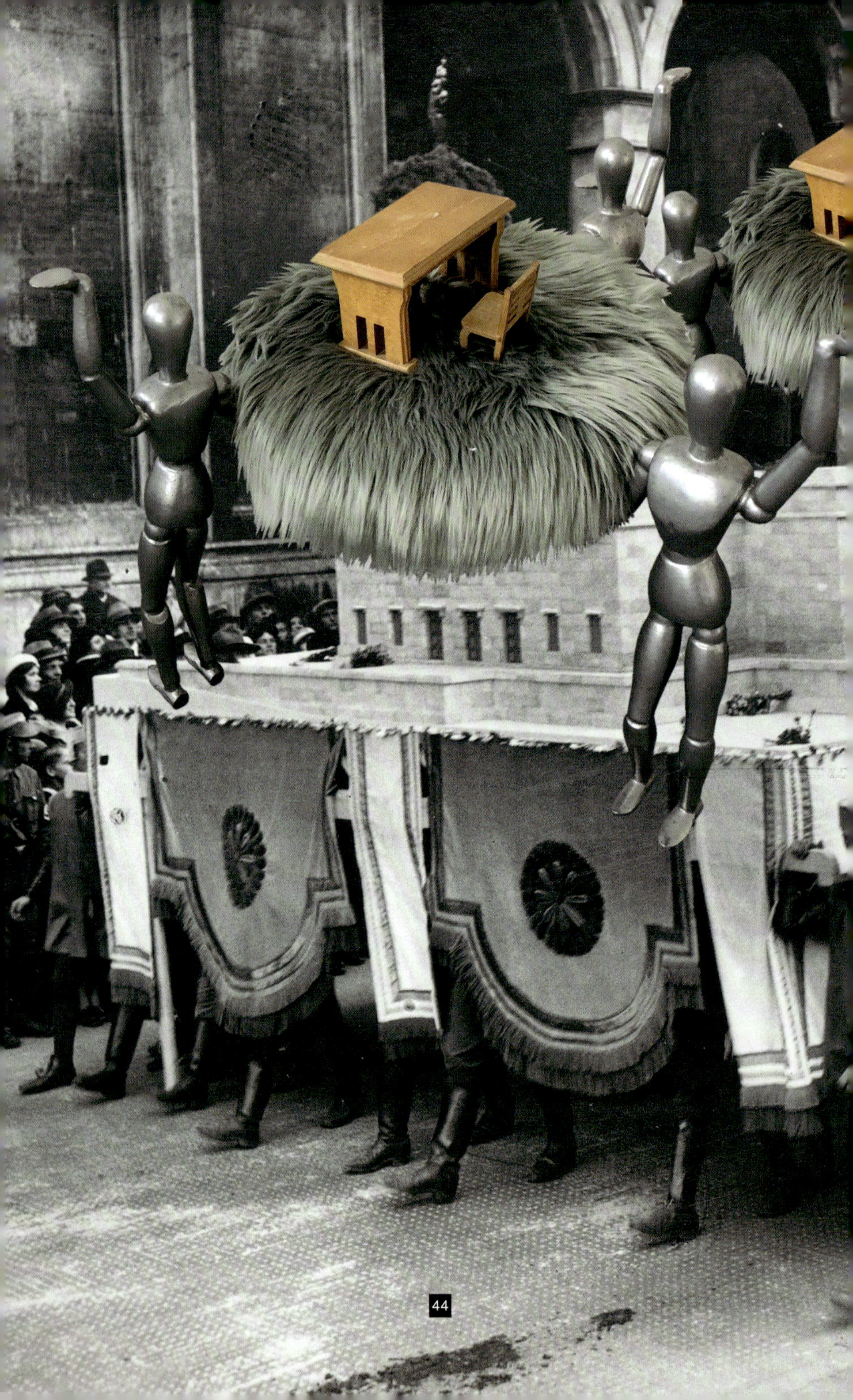

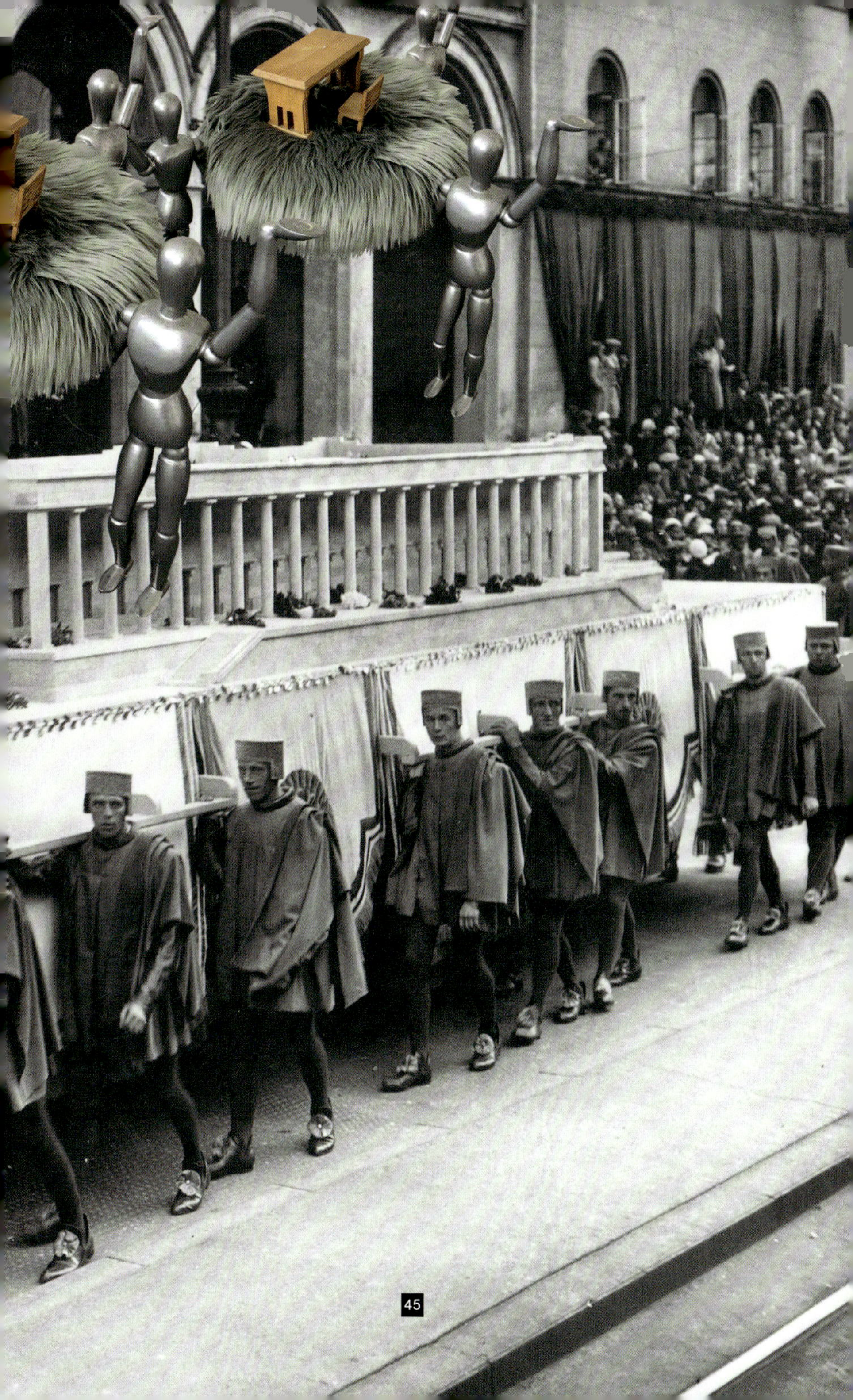

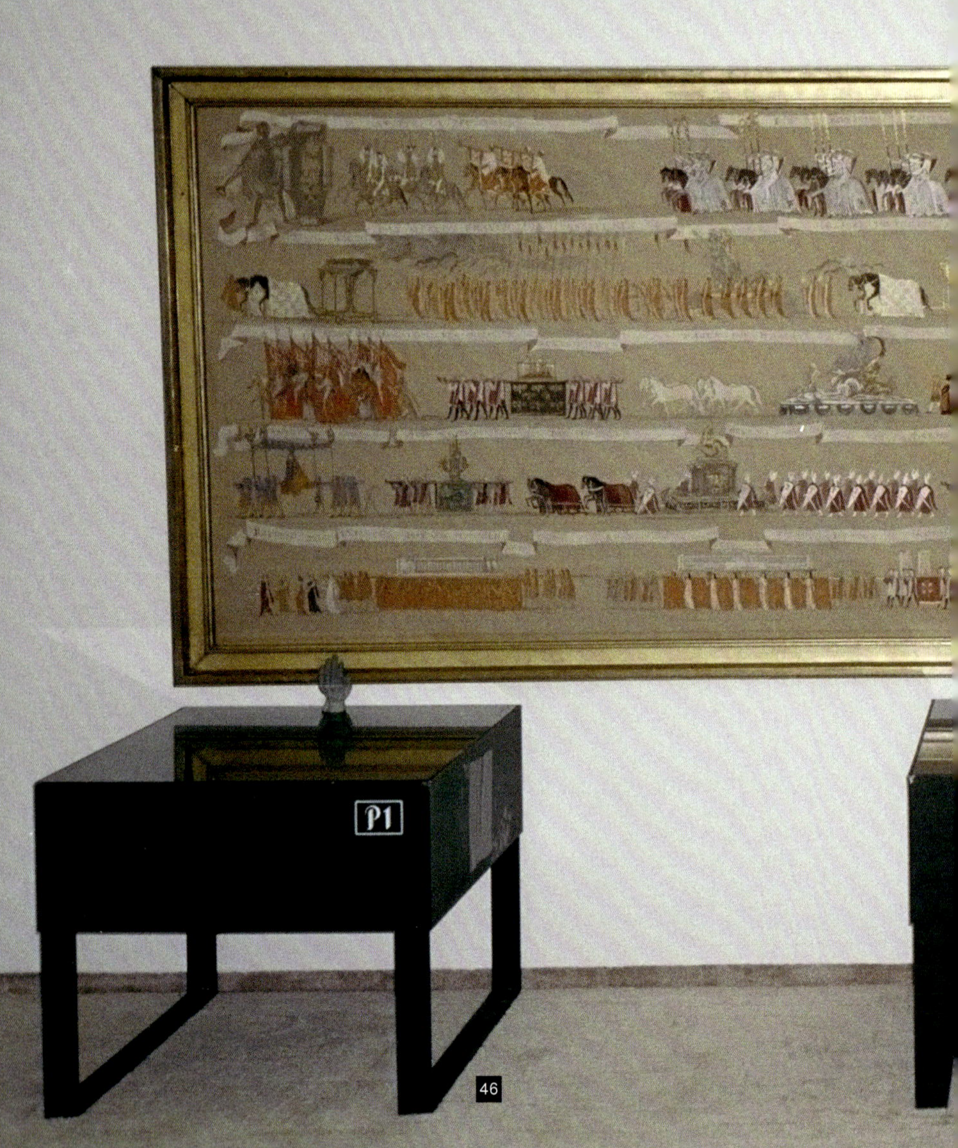
P1

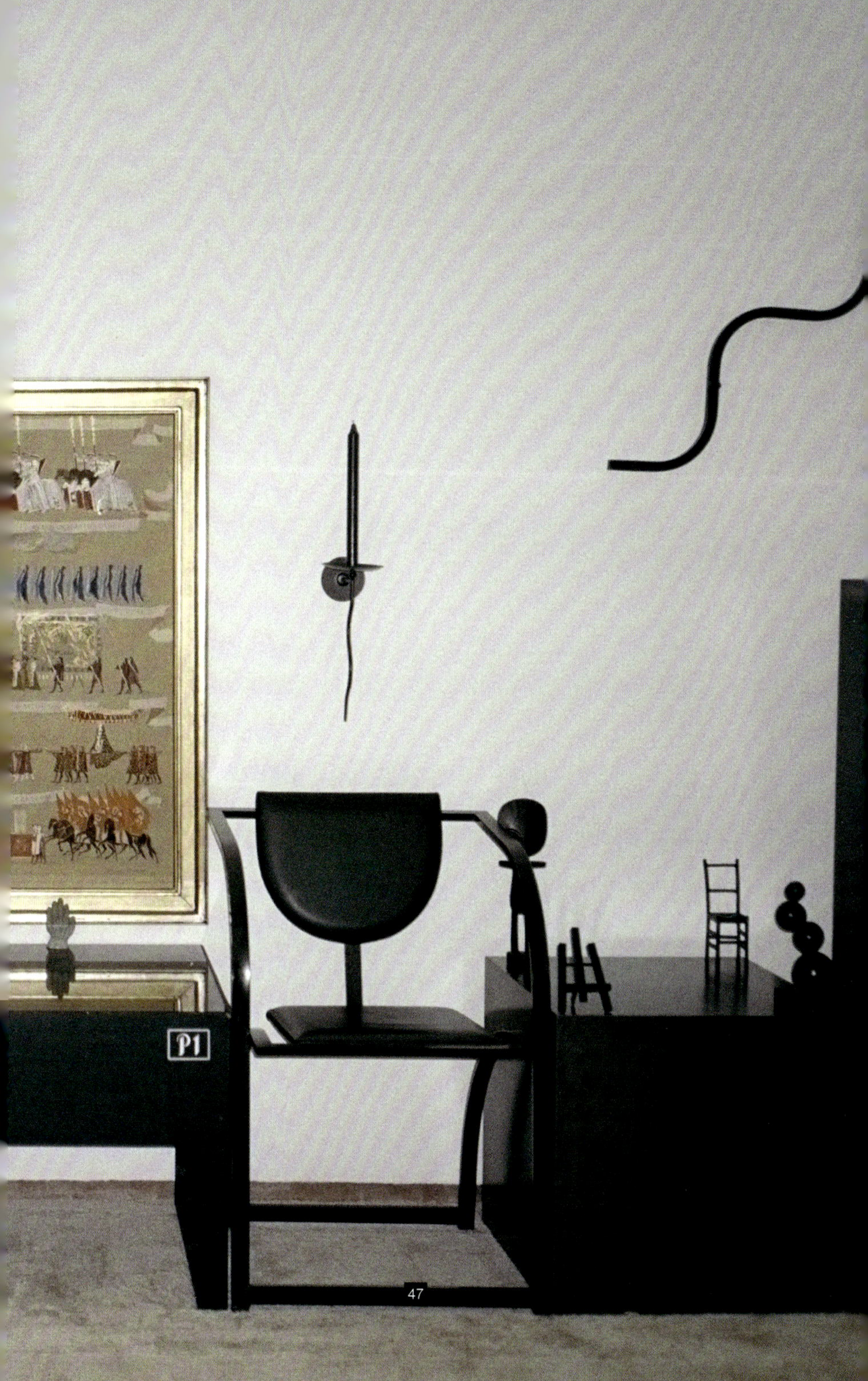
P1

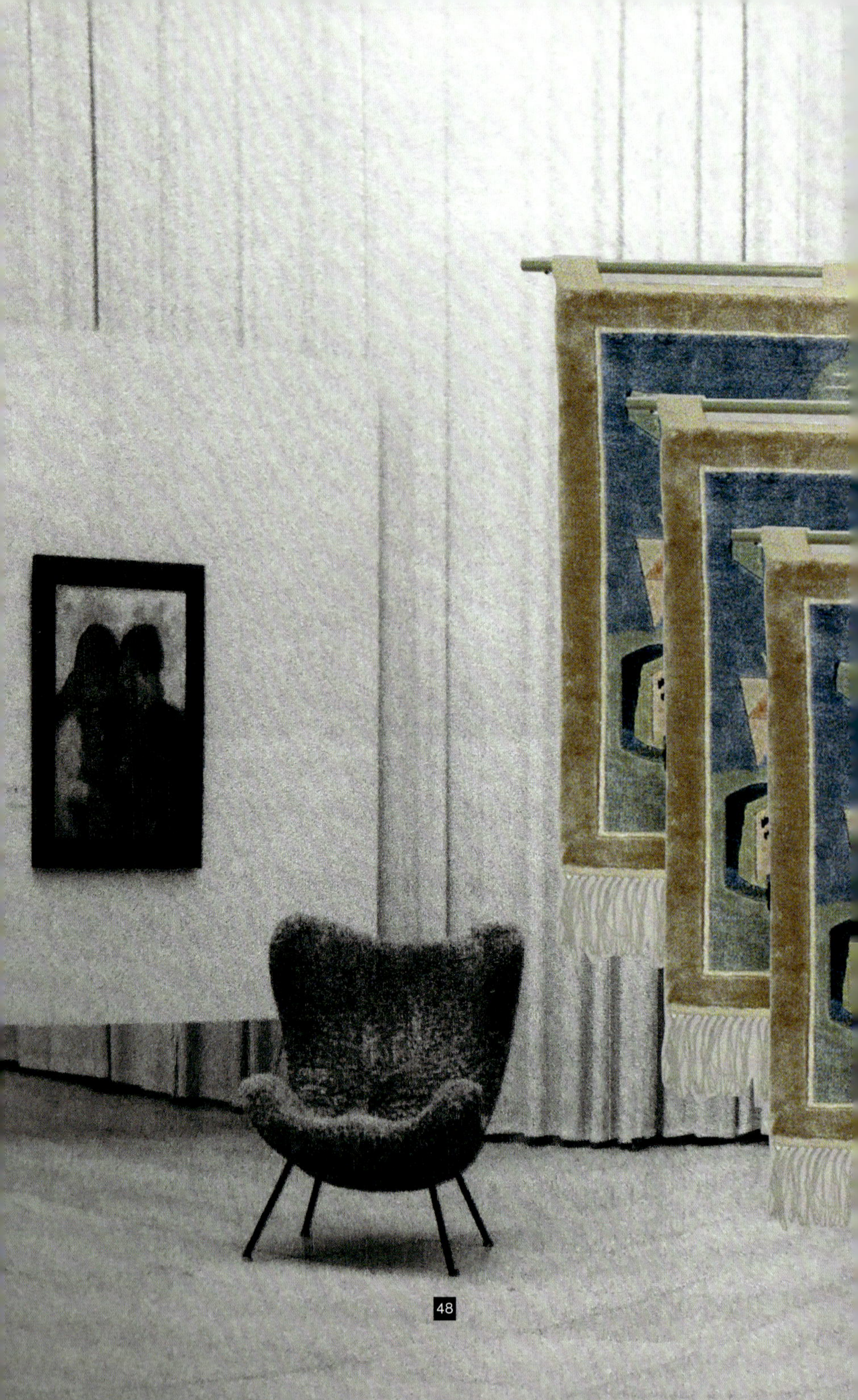

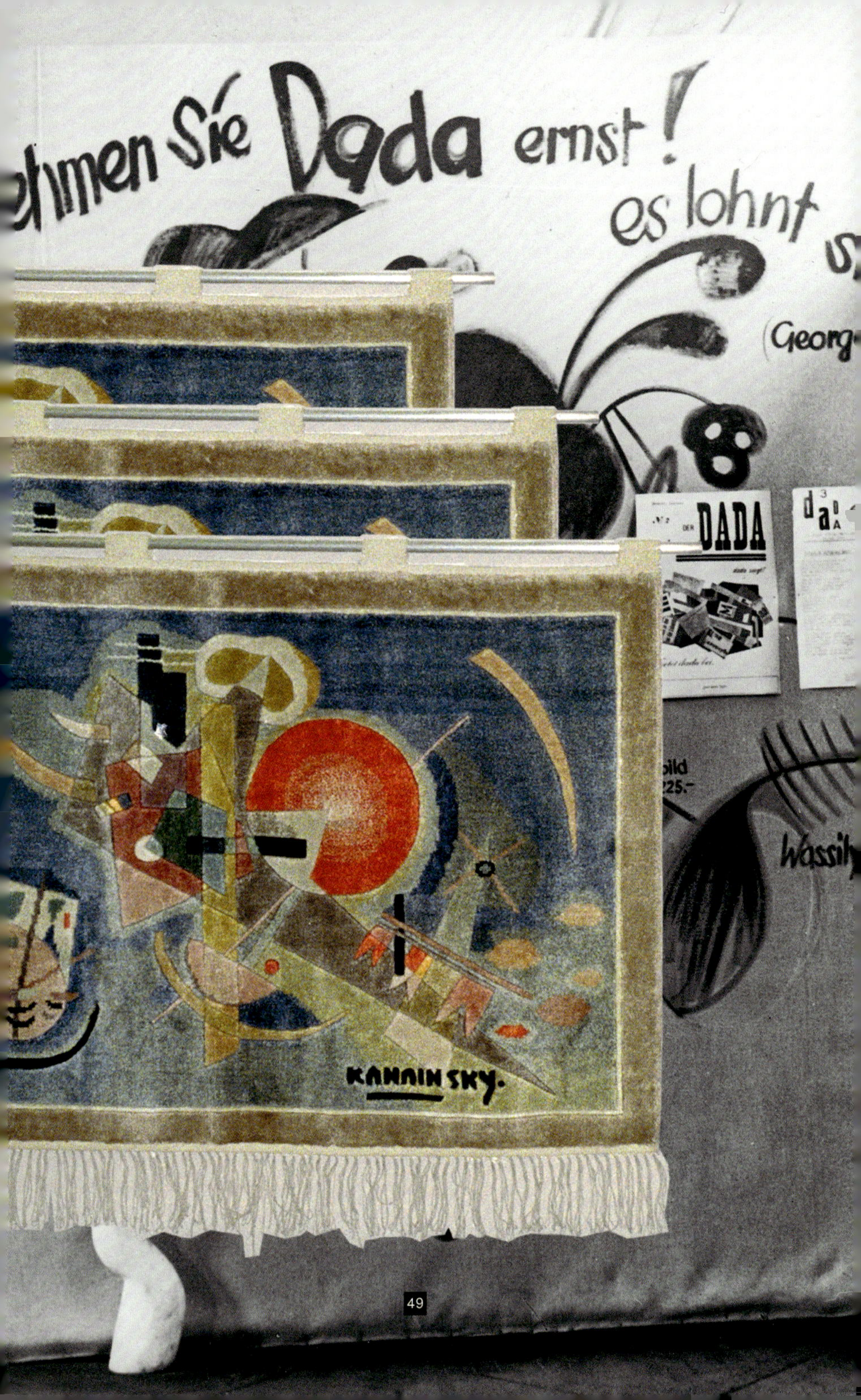

ehmen Sie Dada ernst!
es lohnt s
(Georg
DADA
Bild
225.-
Wassily
KANDINSKY.

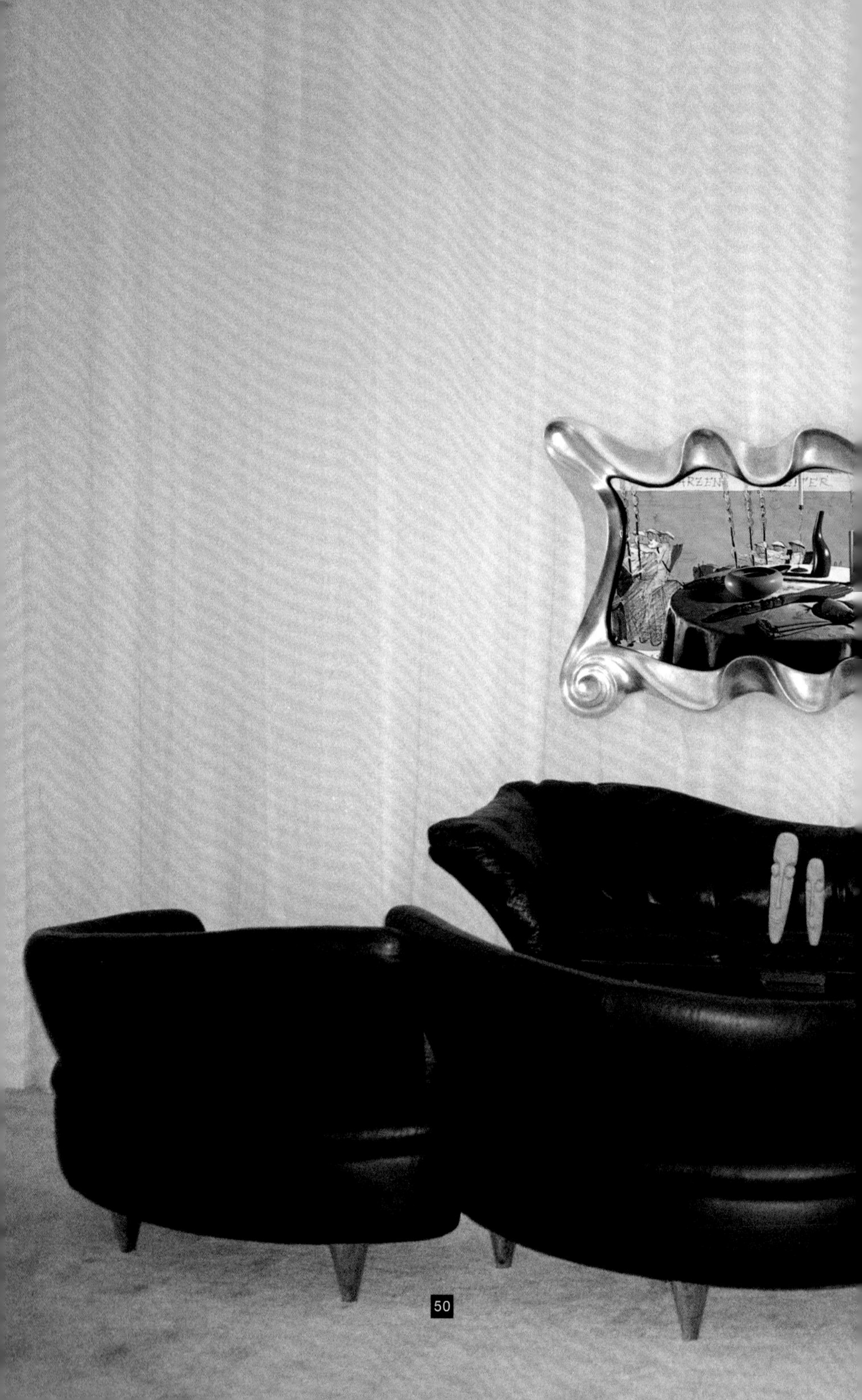

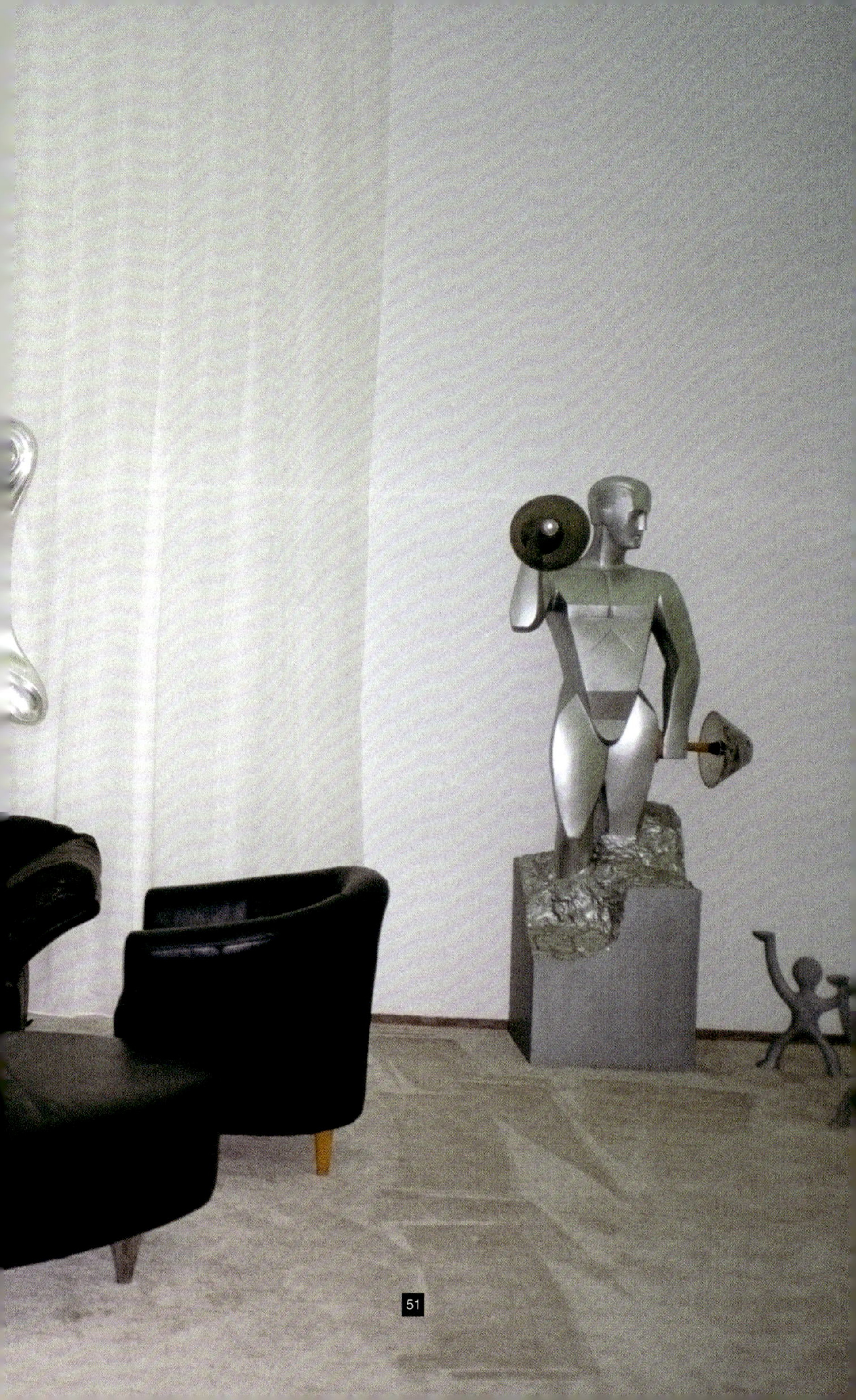

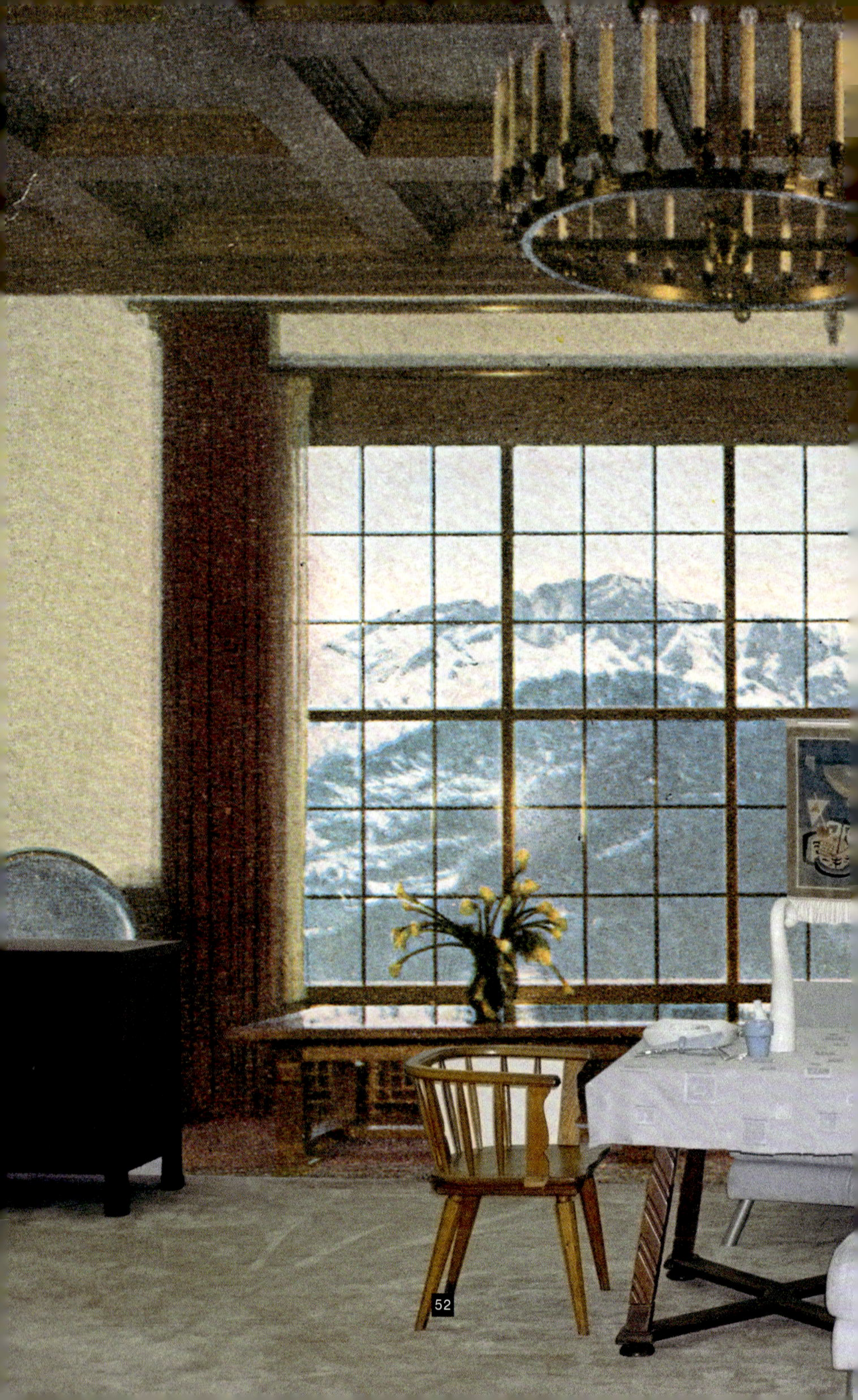

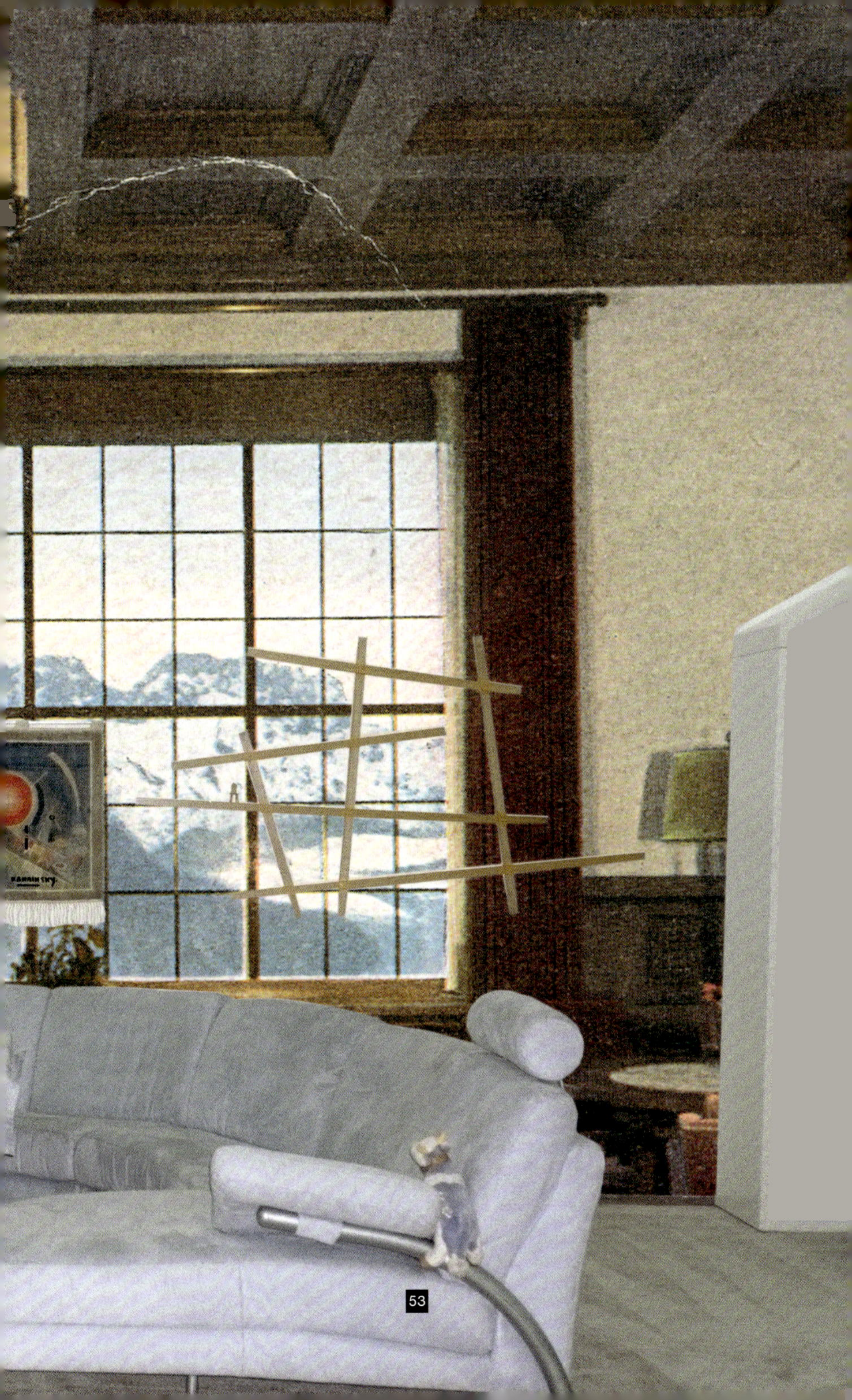

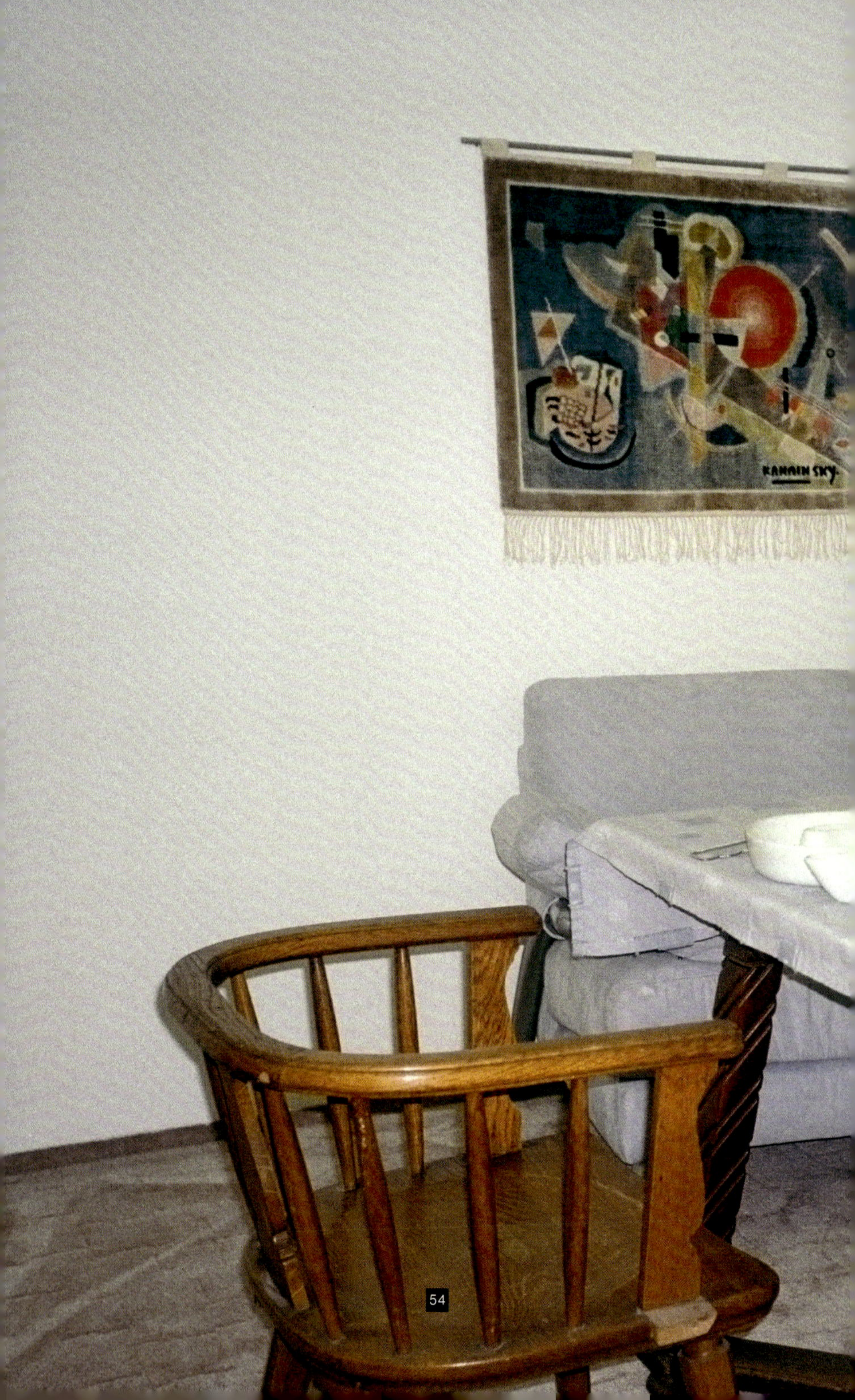

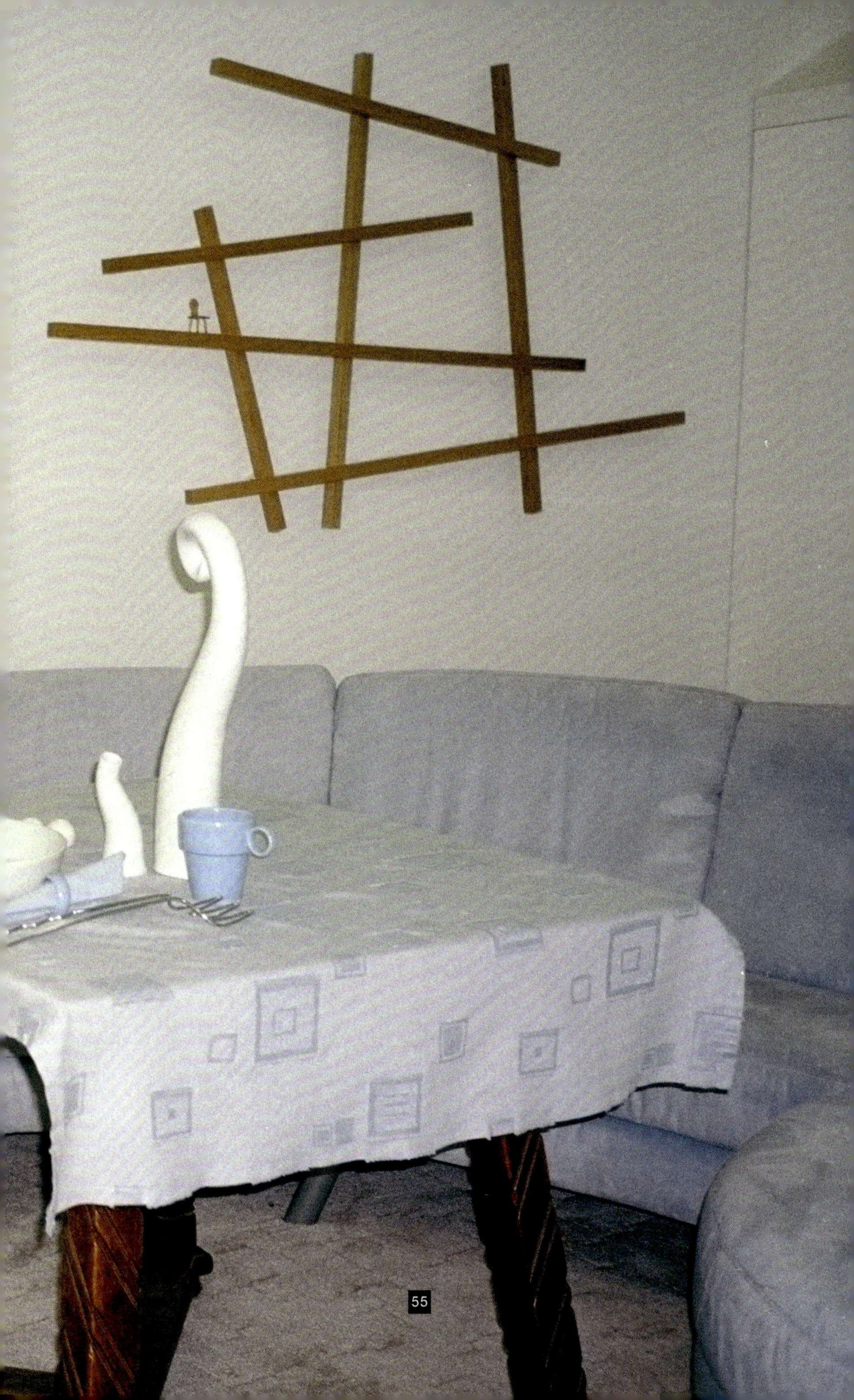

Haus Berghof
Große Halle

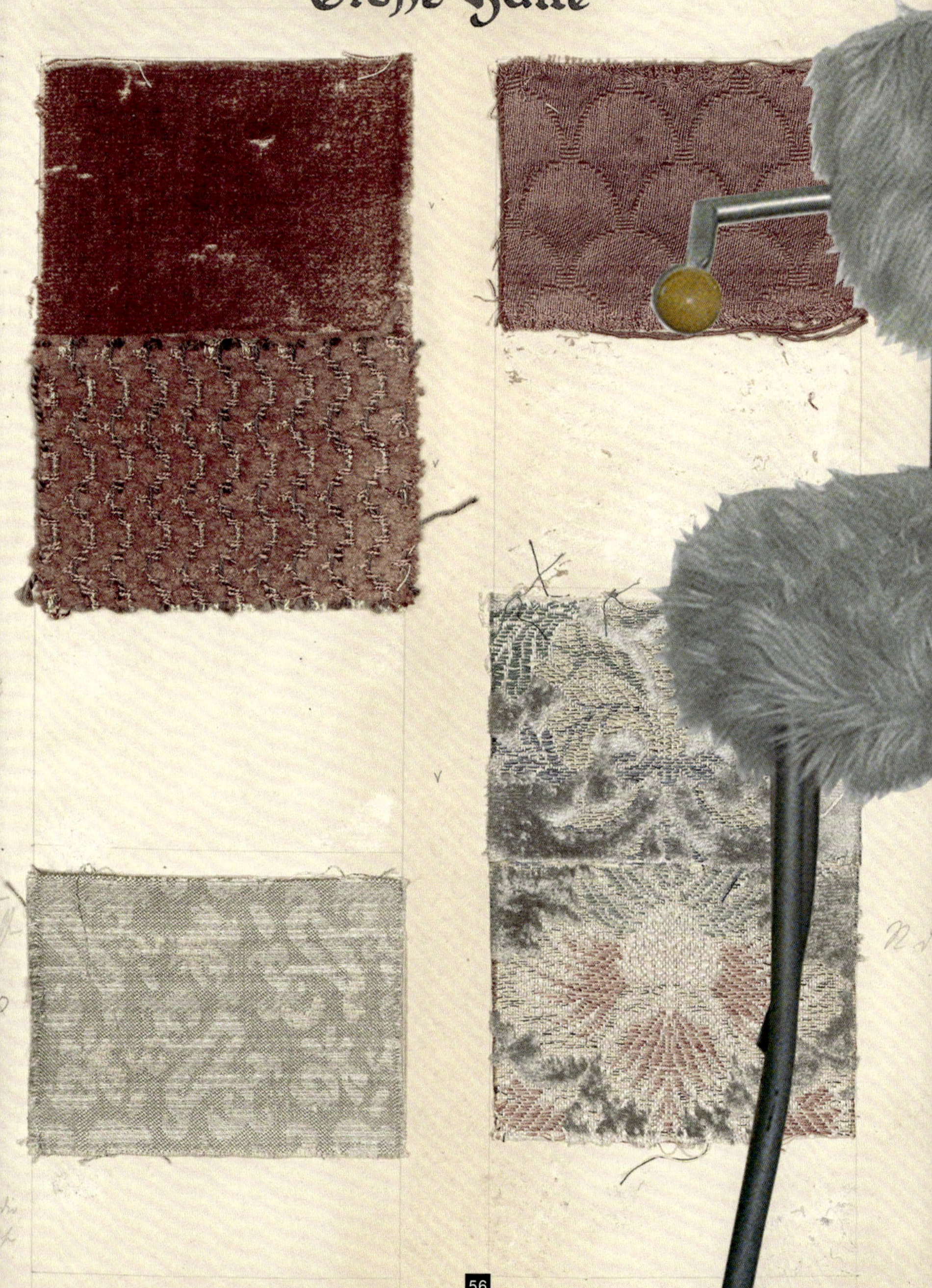

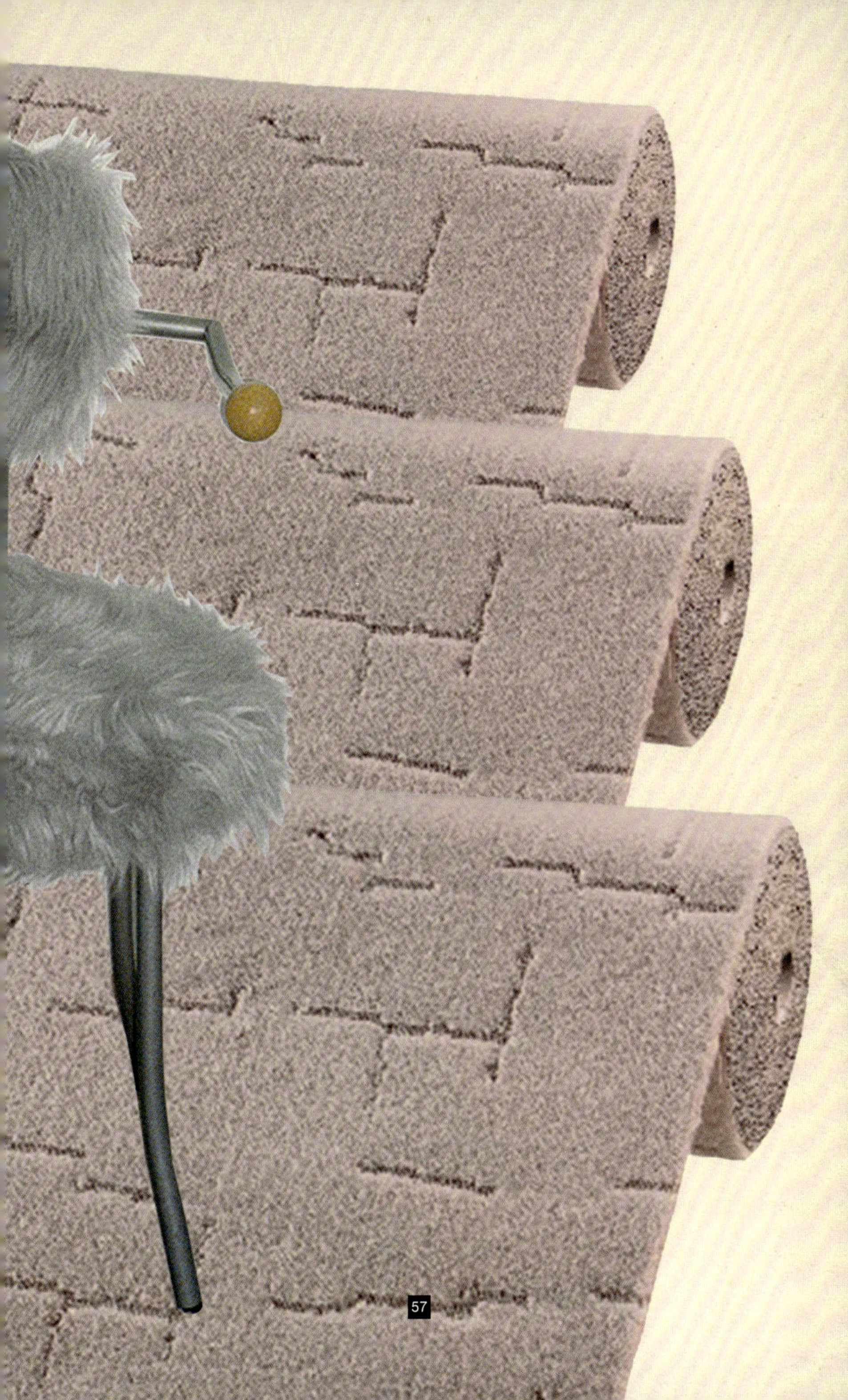

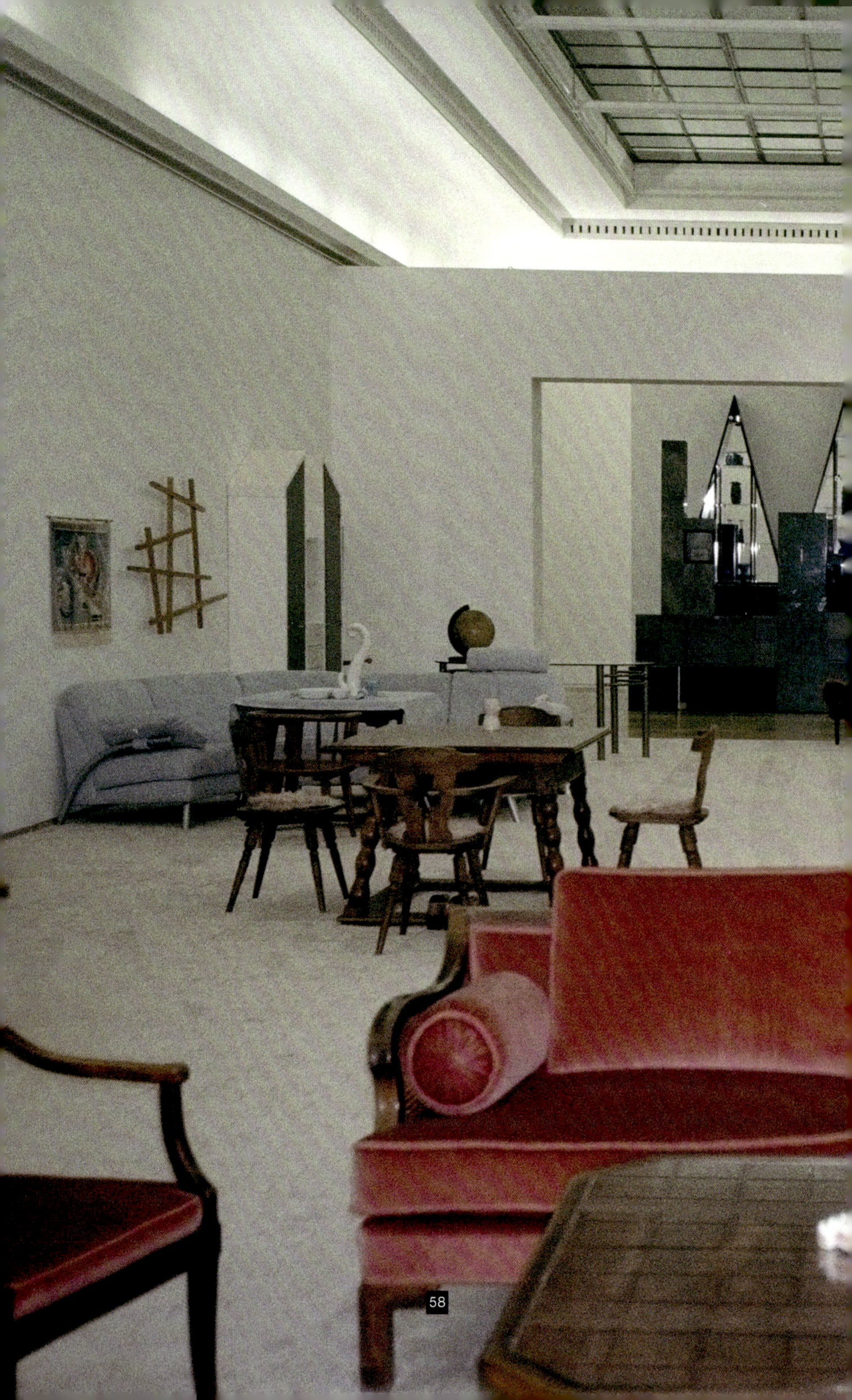

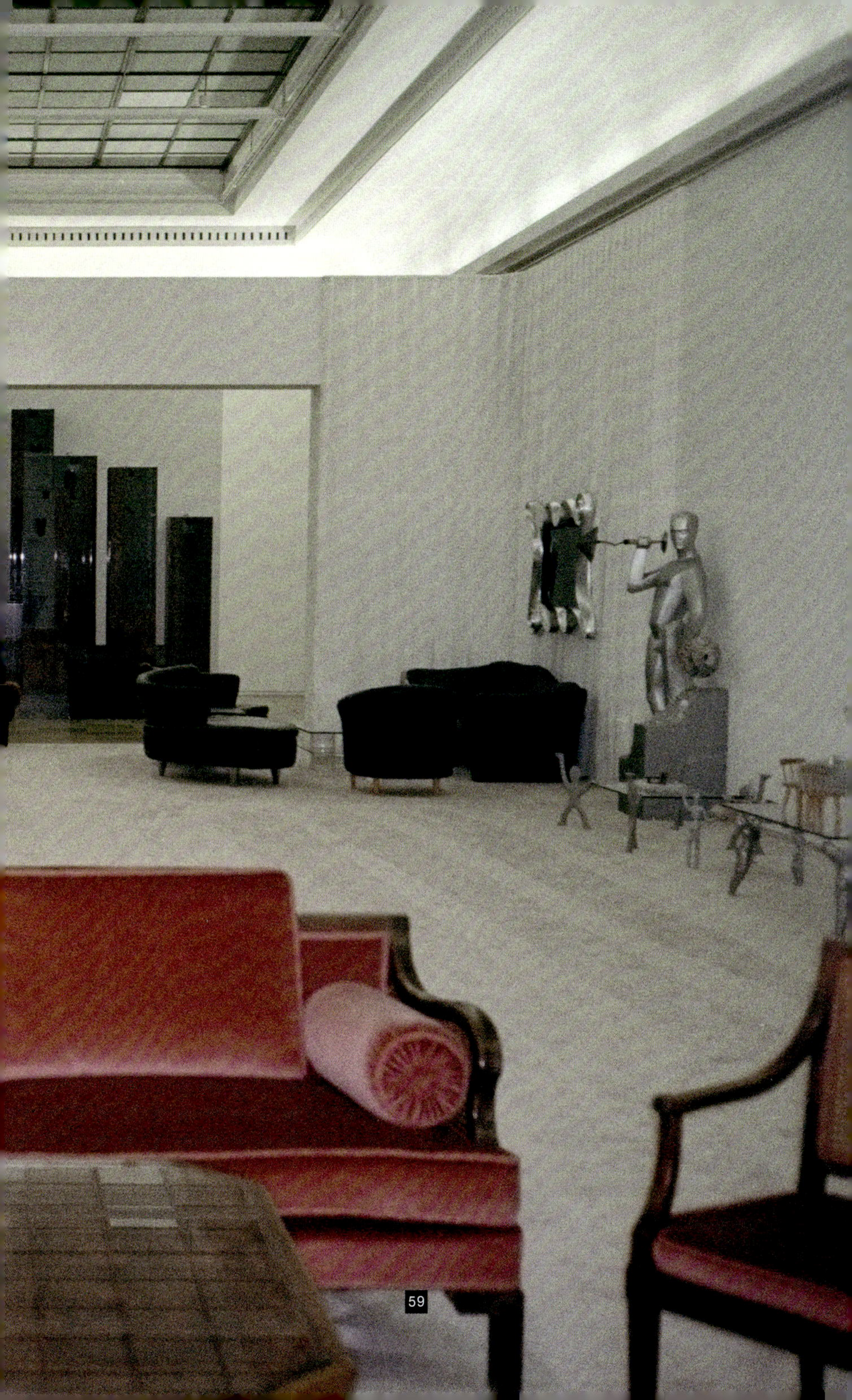

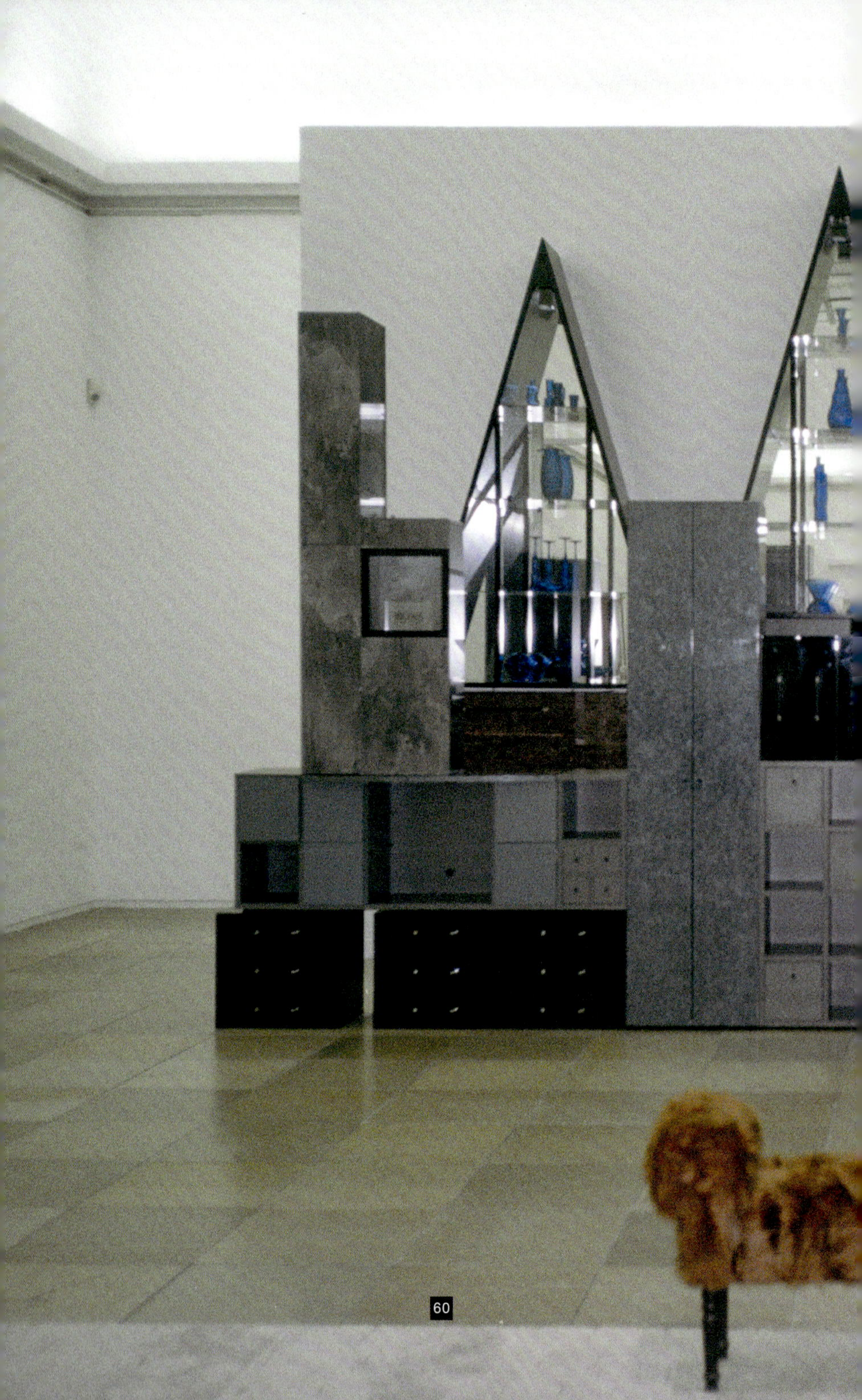

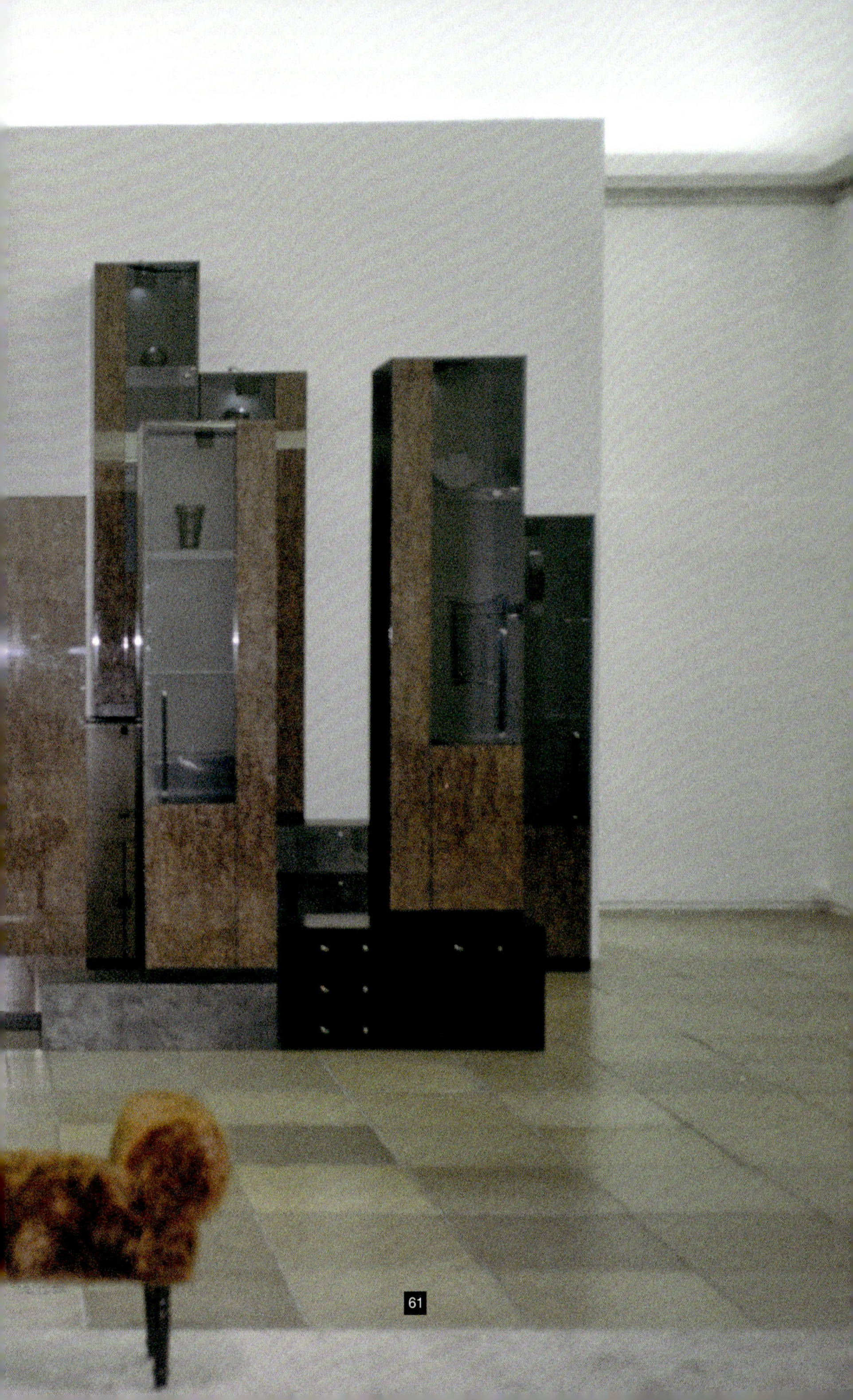

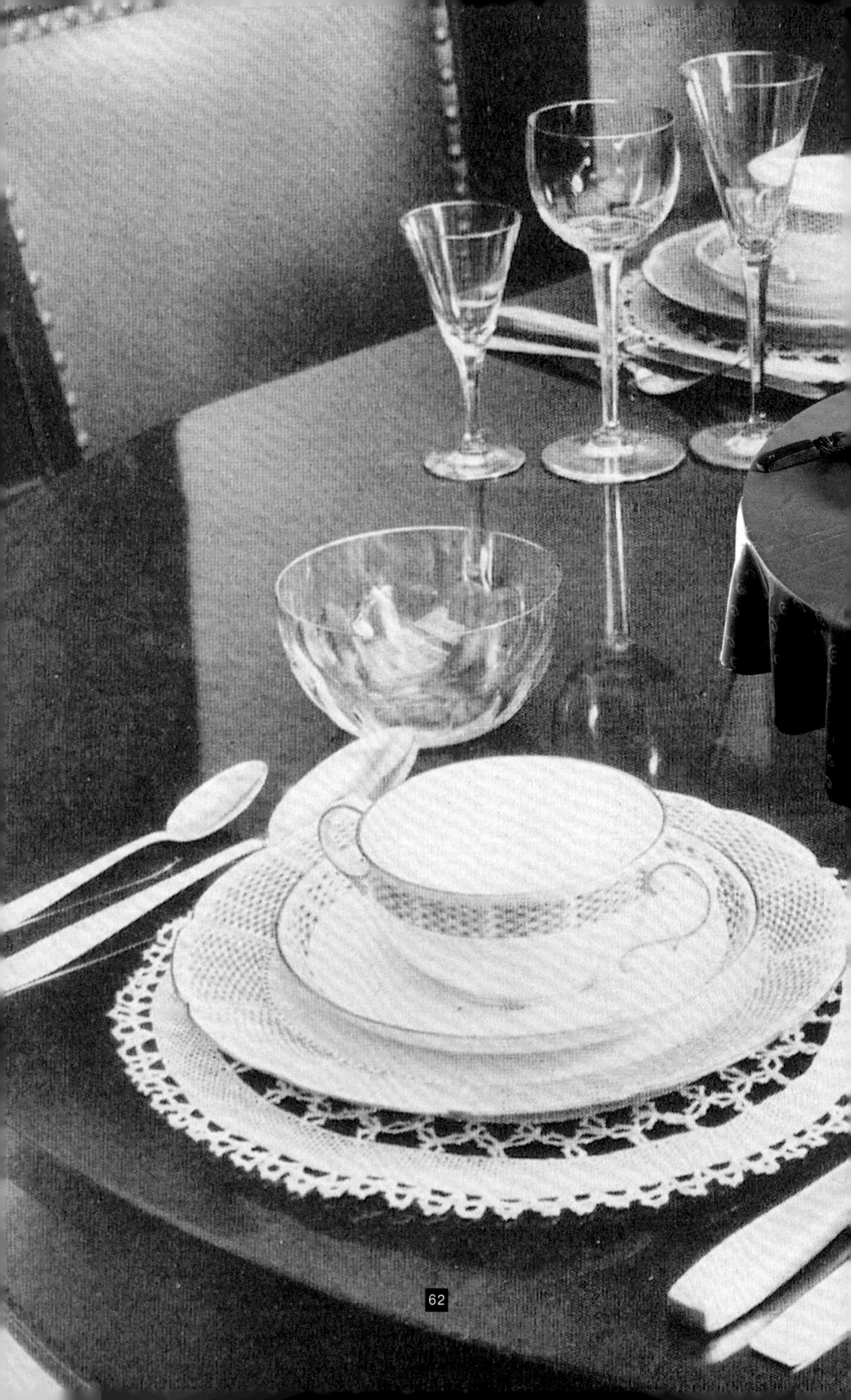

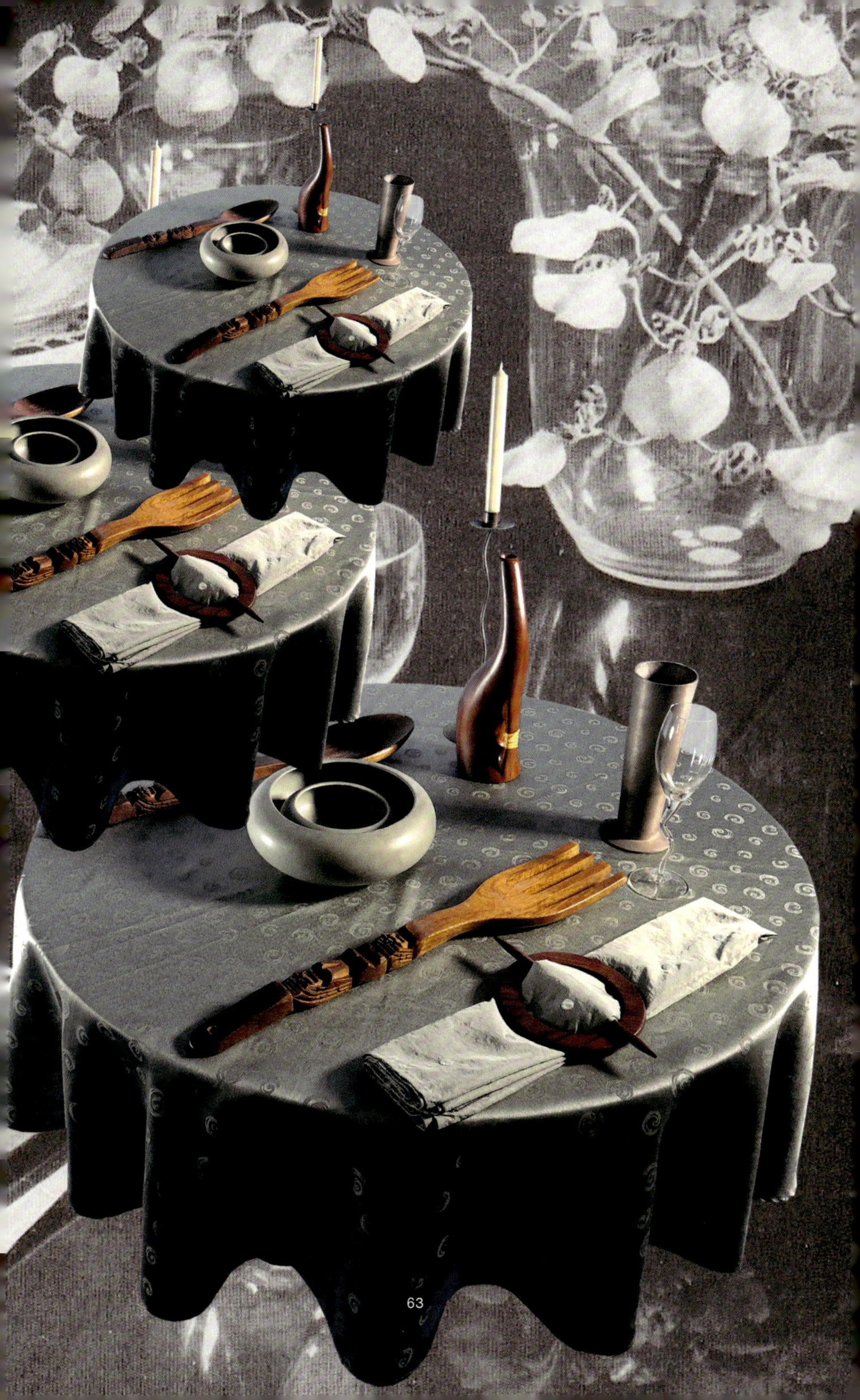

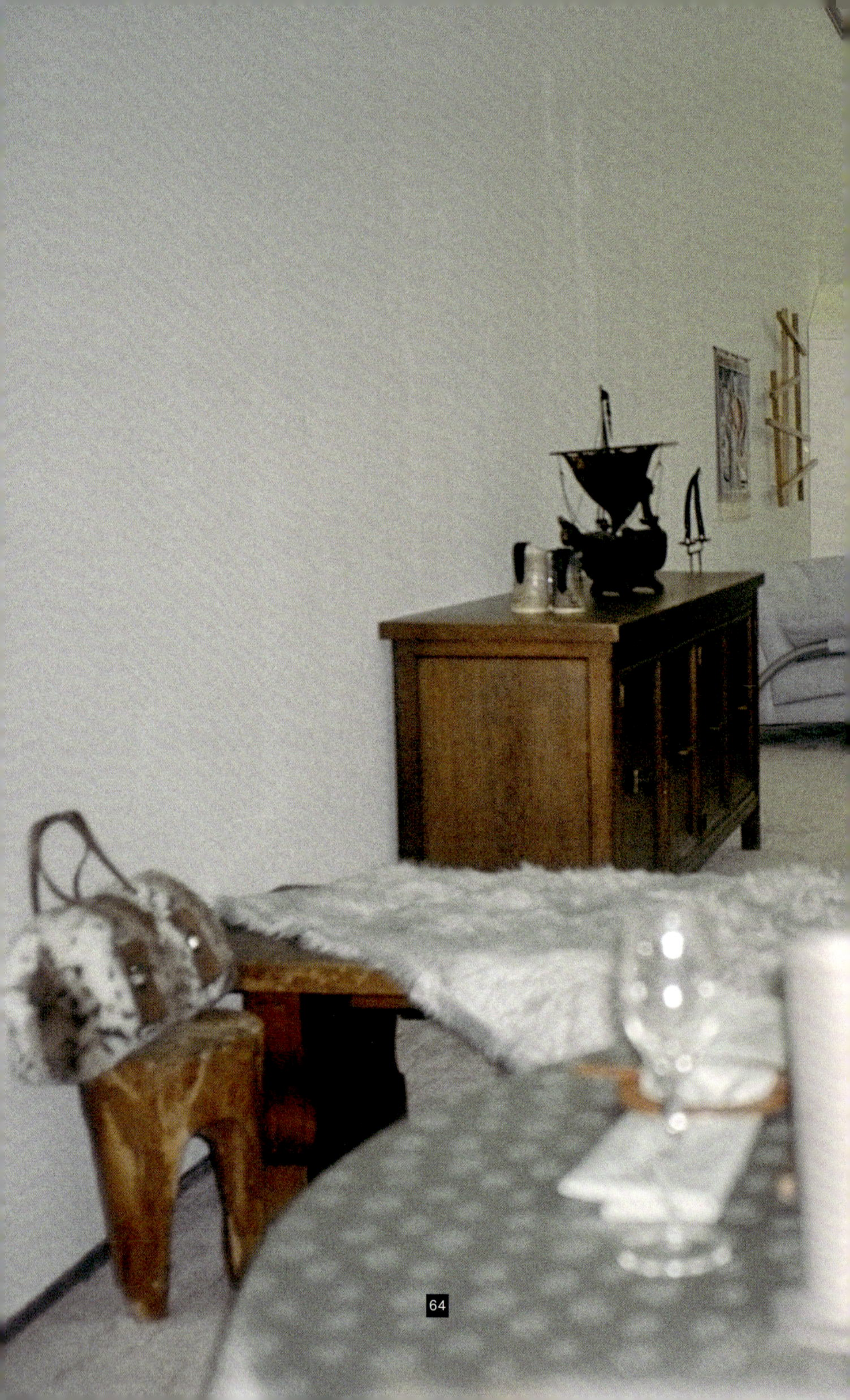

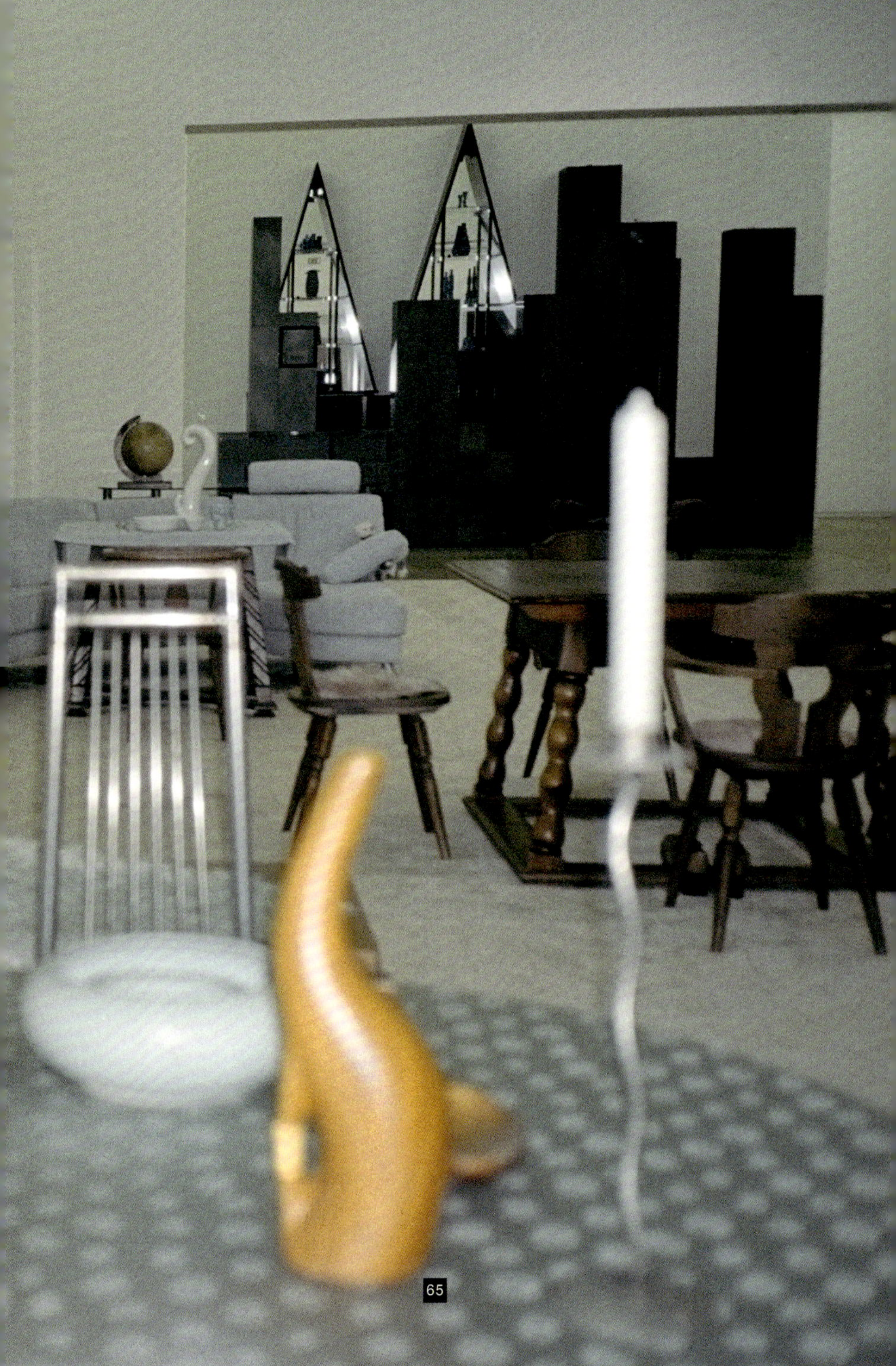

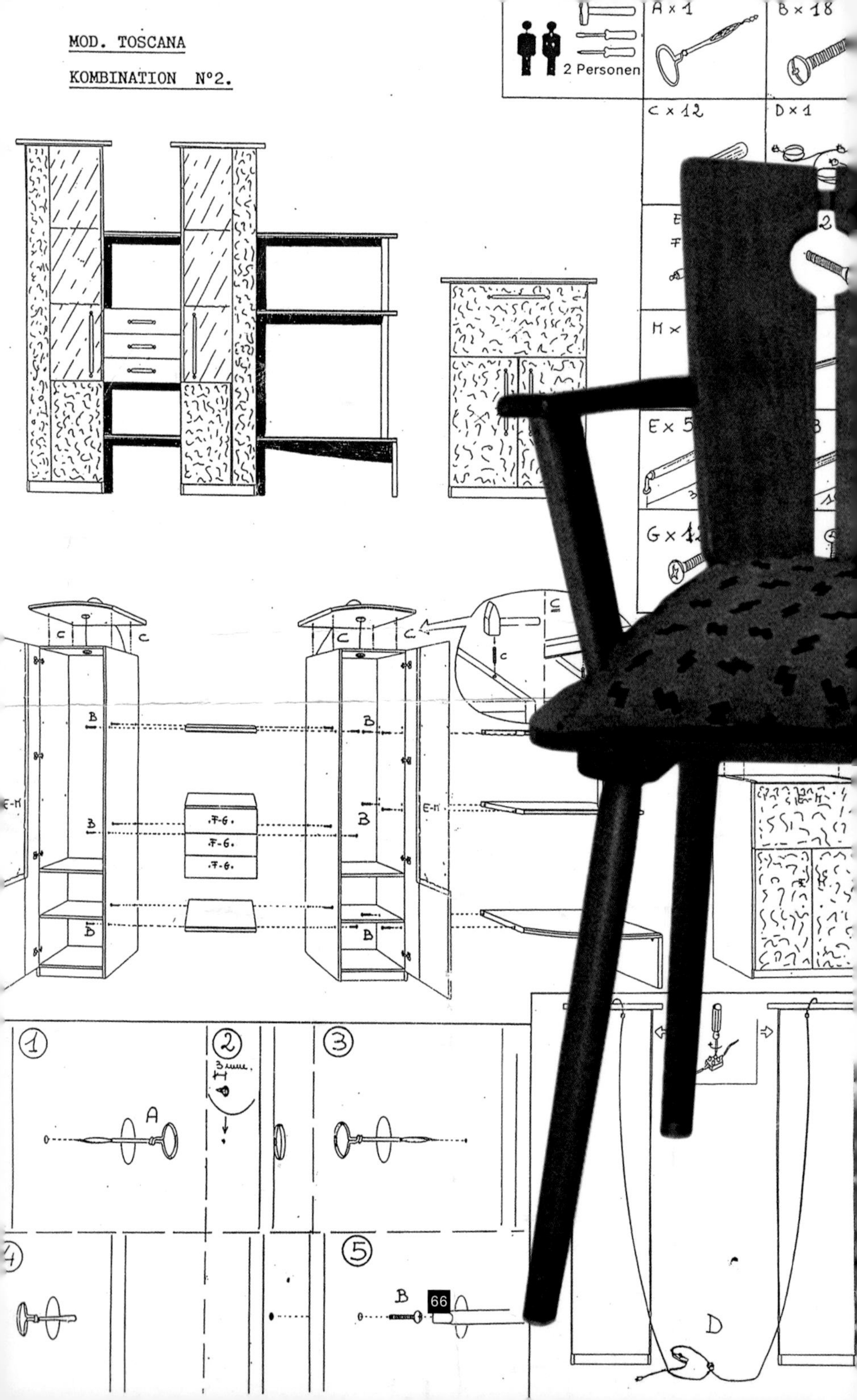
MOD. TOSCANA
KOMBINATION N°2.
2 Personen
A × 1
B × 18
C × 12
D × 1
G × 12
C
B
E-M
F-G
1
2
3
4
5
A
D

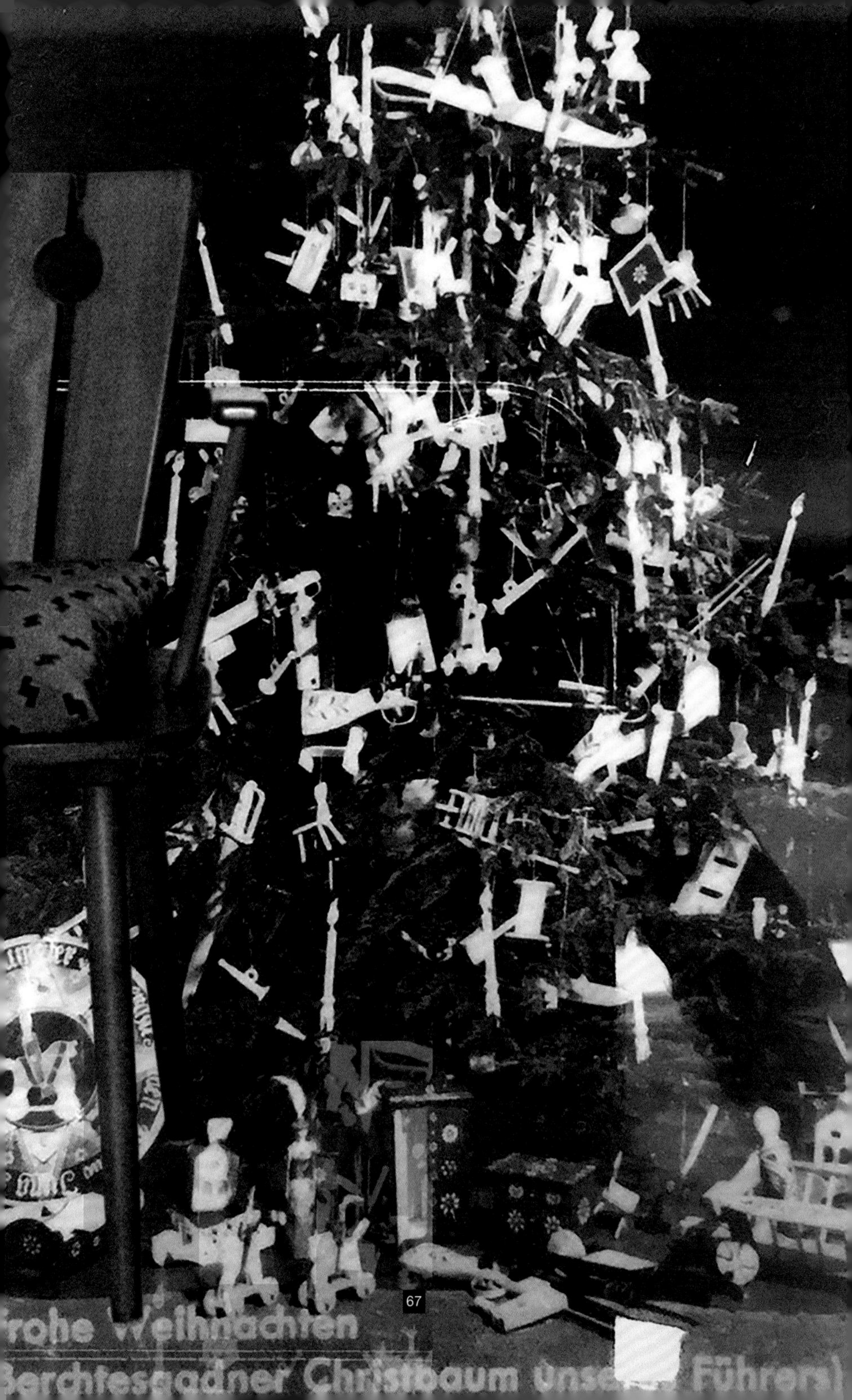
rohe Weihnachten
Berchtesgadner Christbaum unse Führers

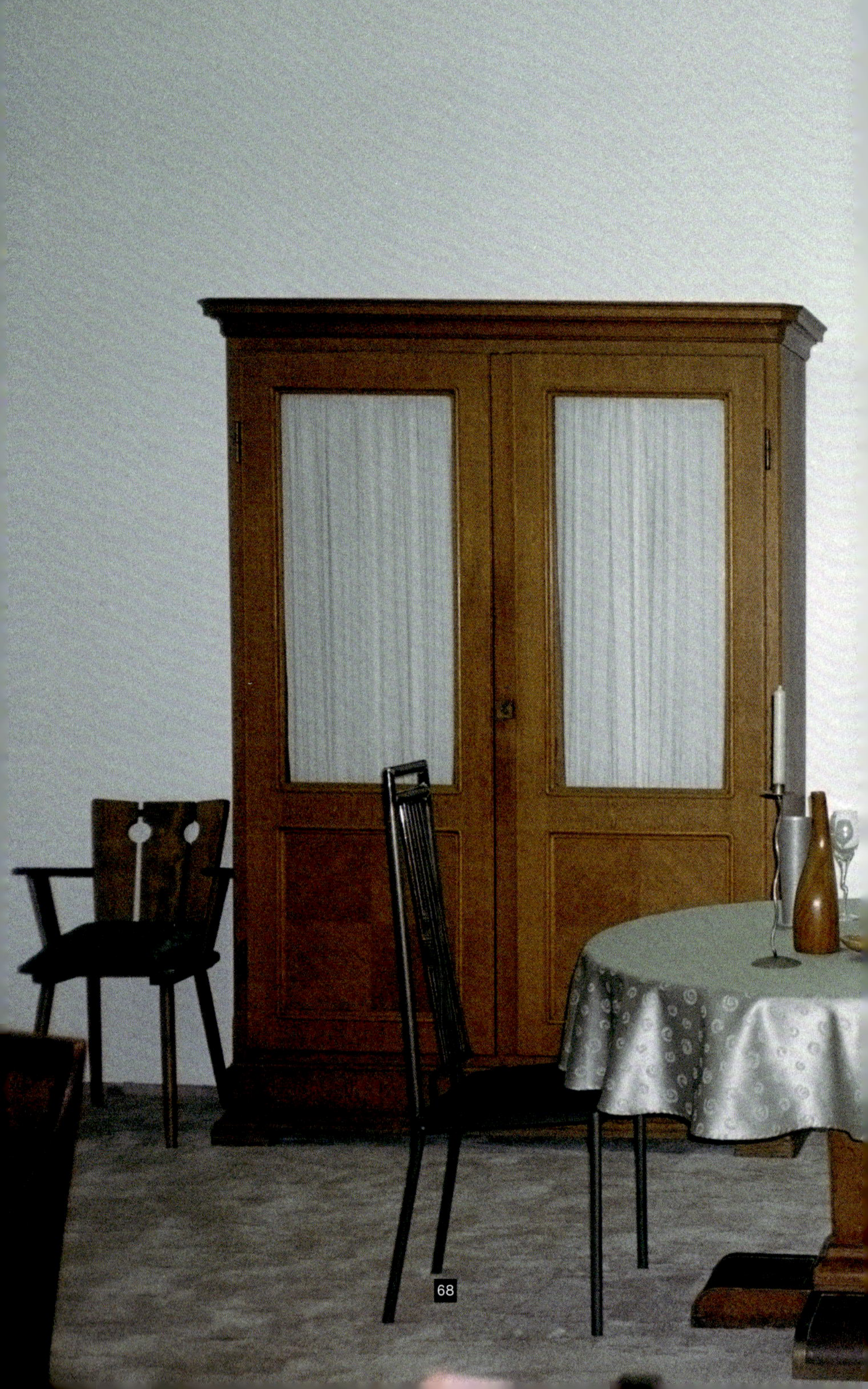

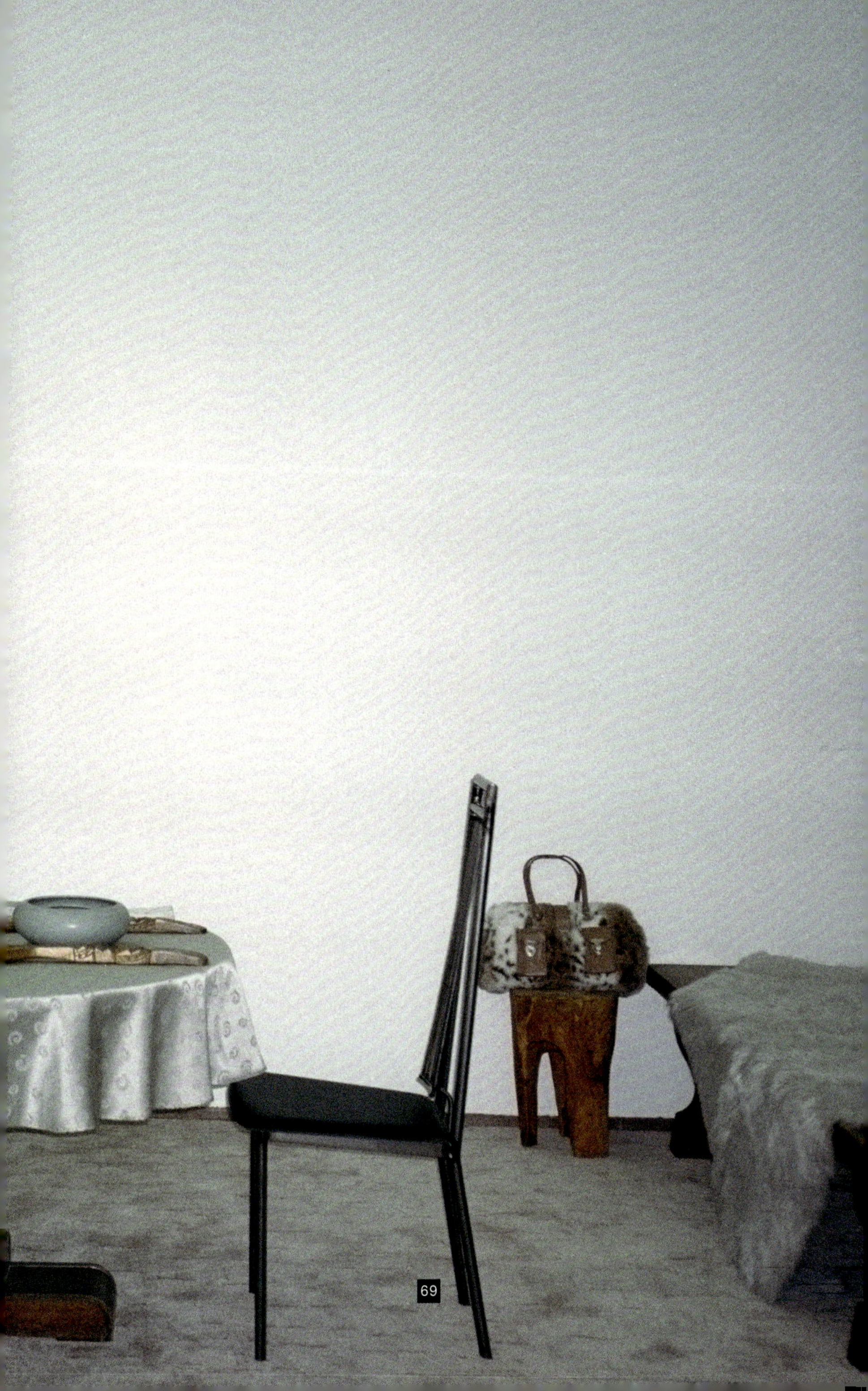

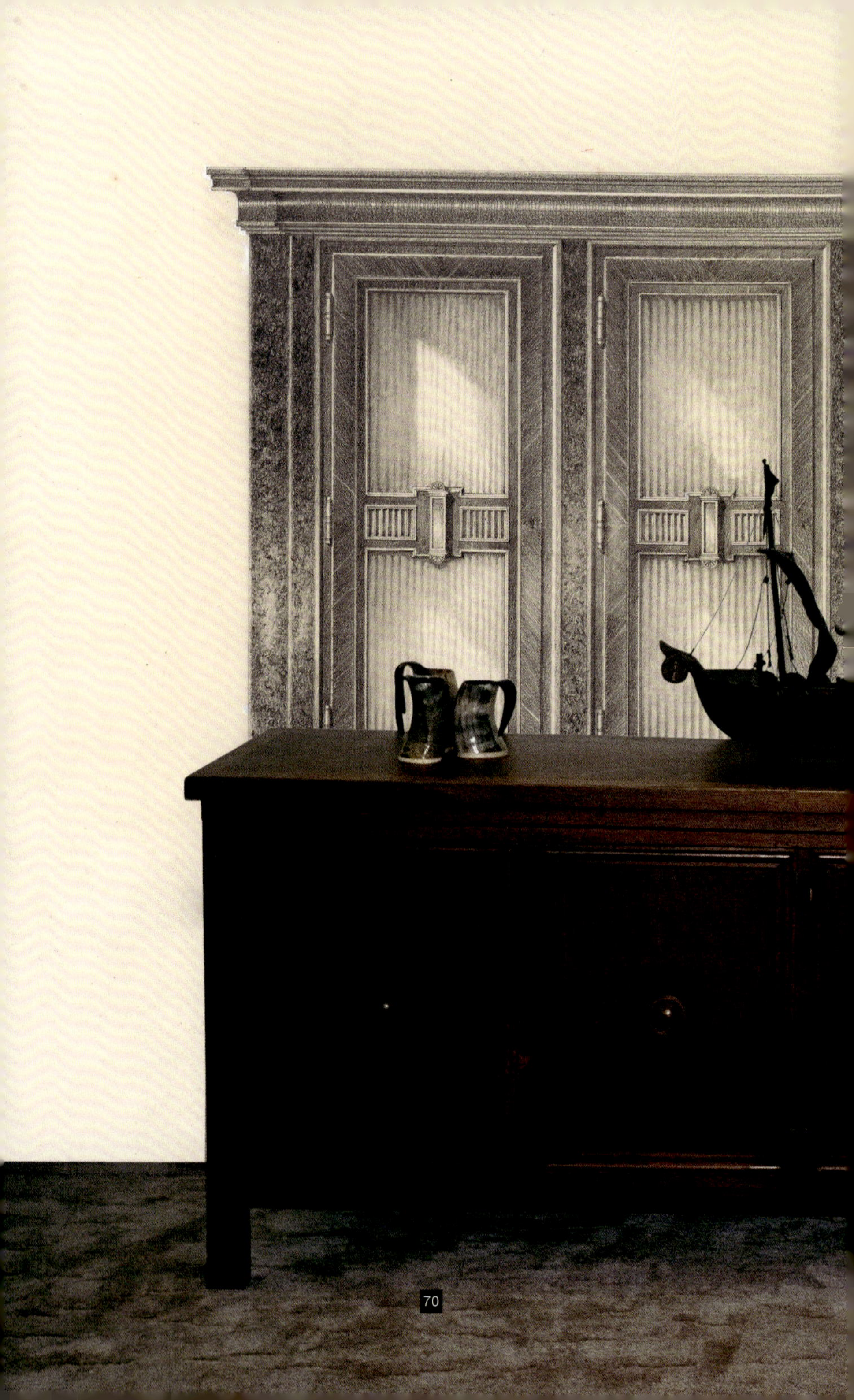

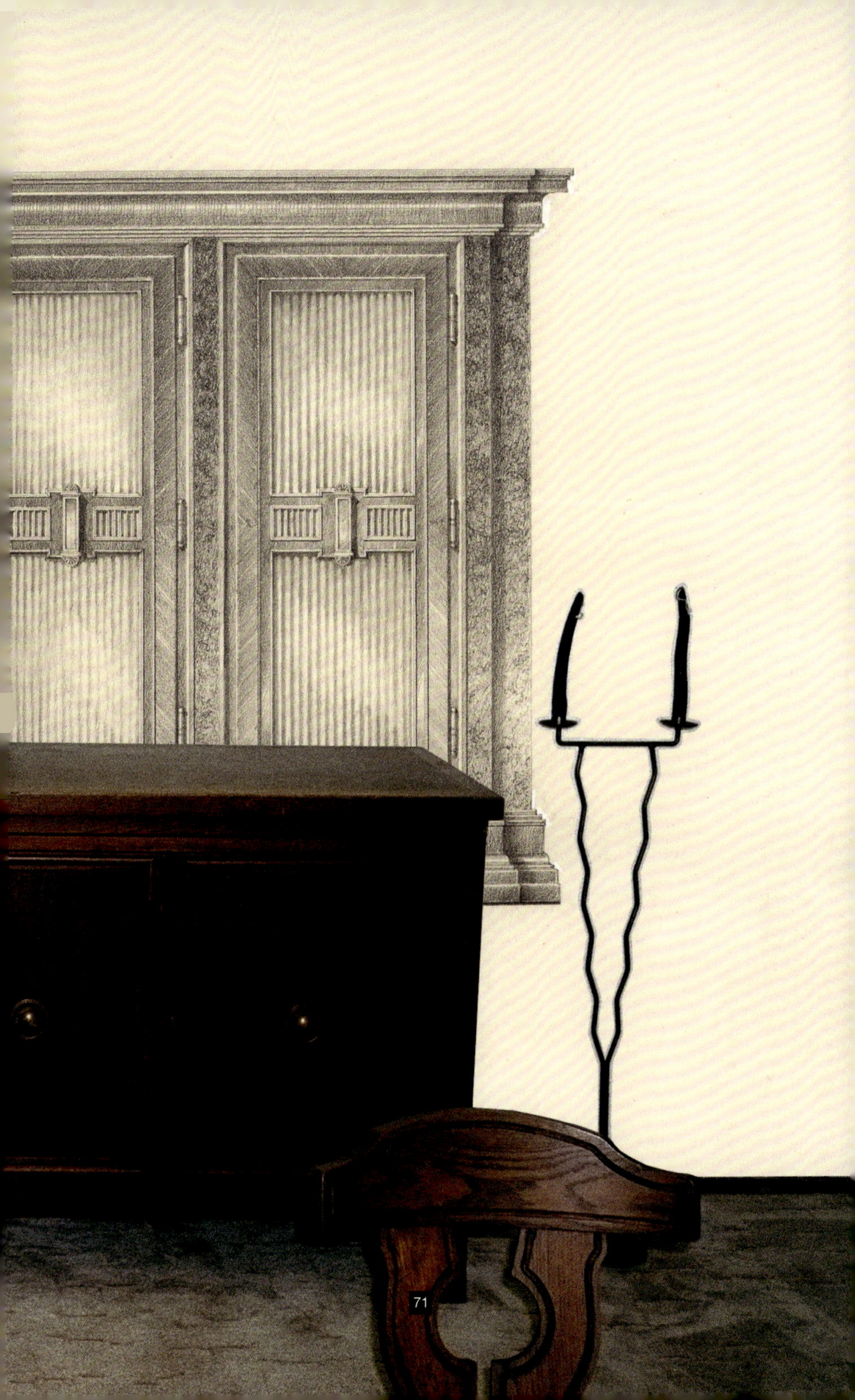

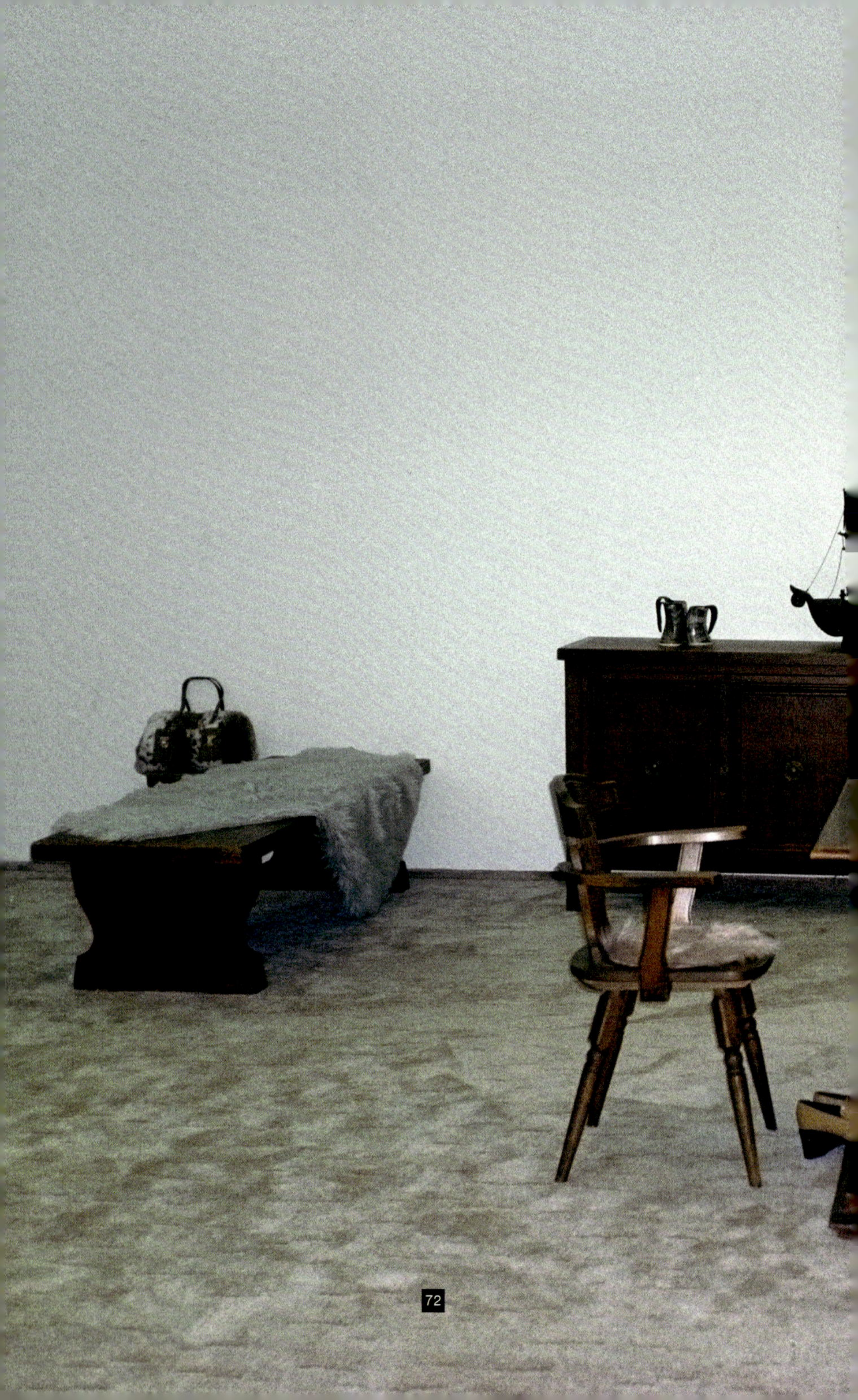

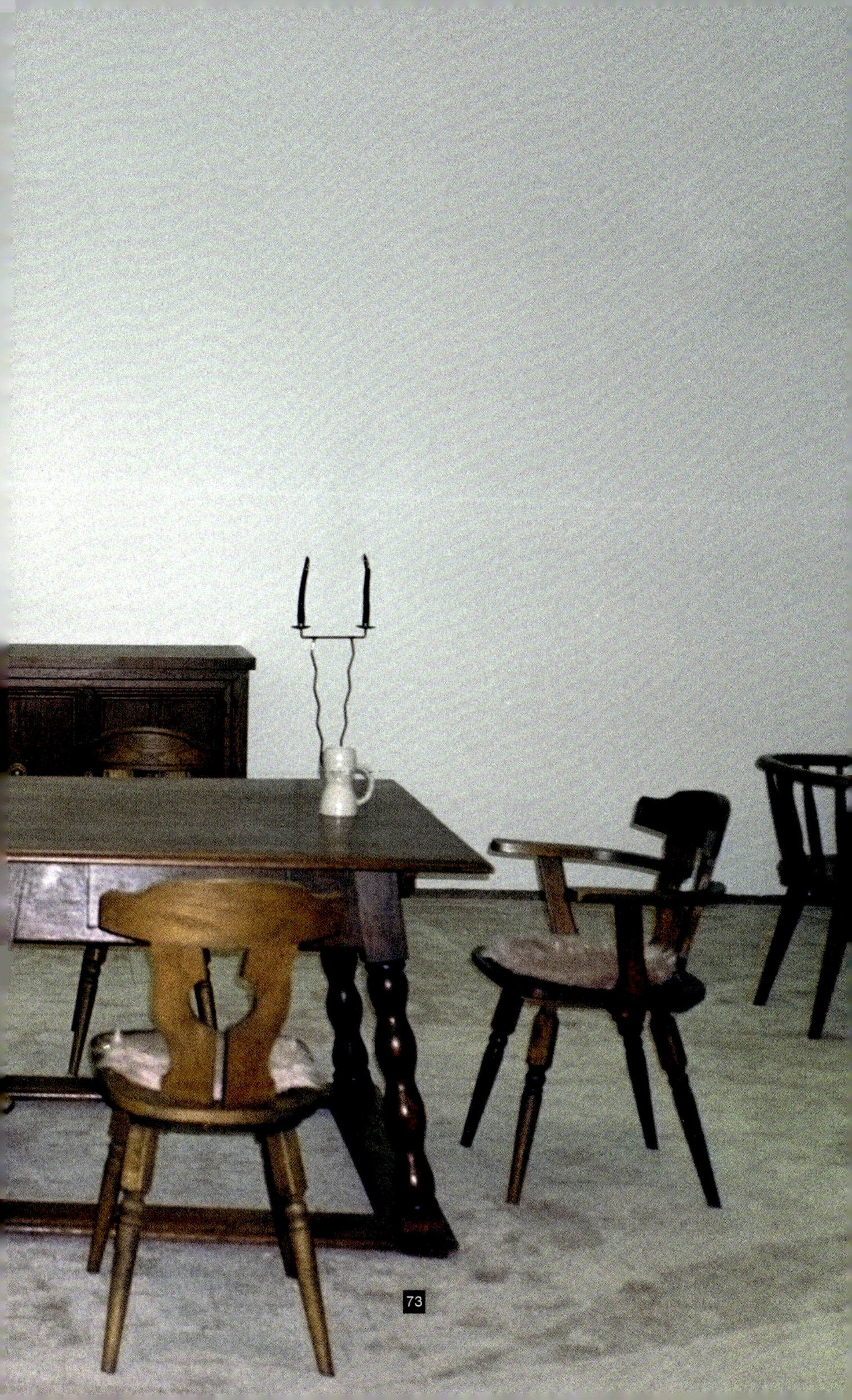

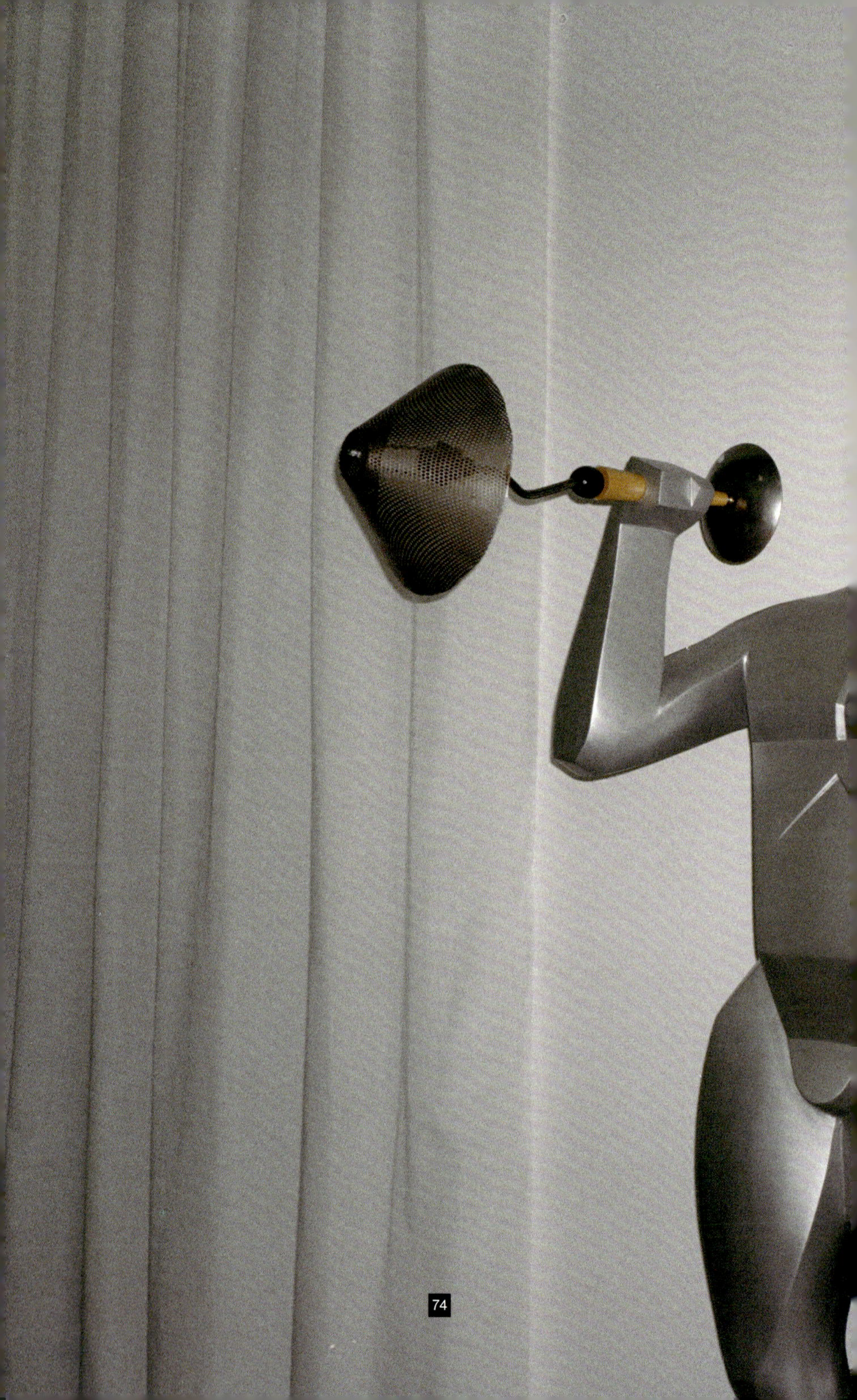

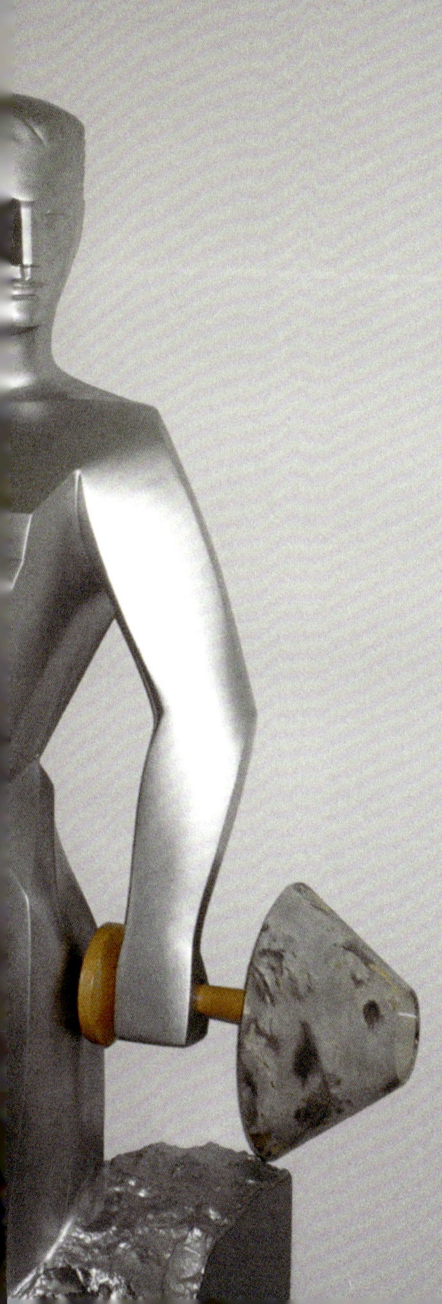

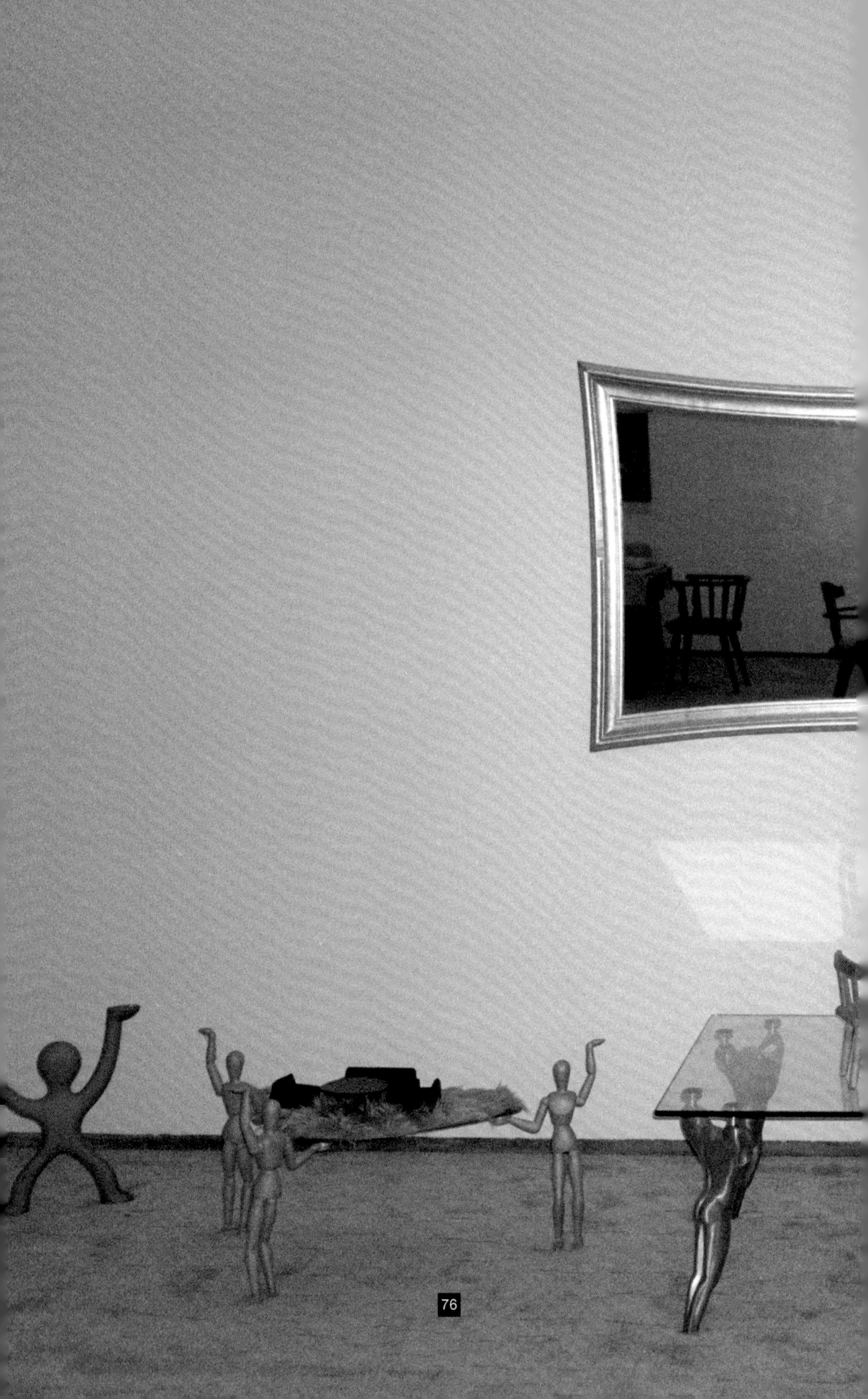

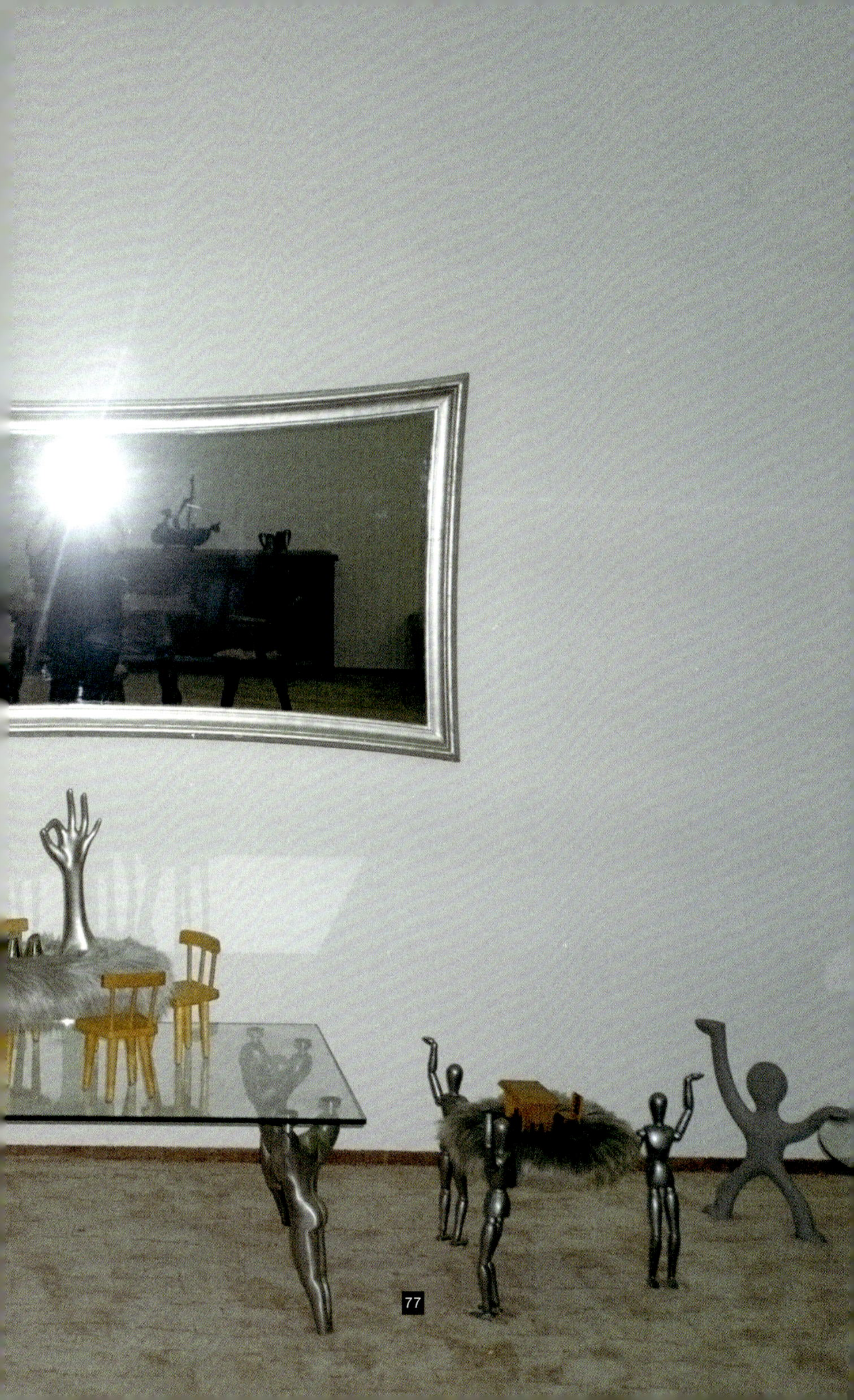

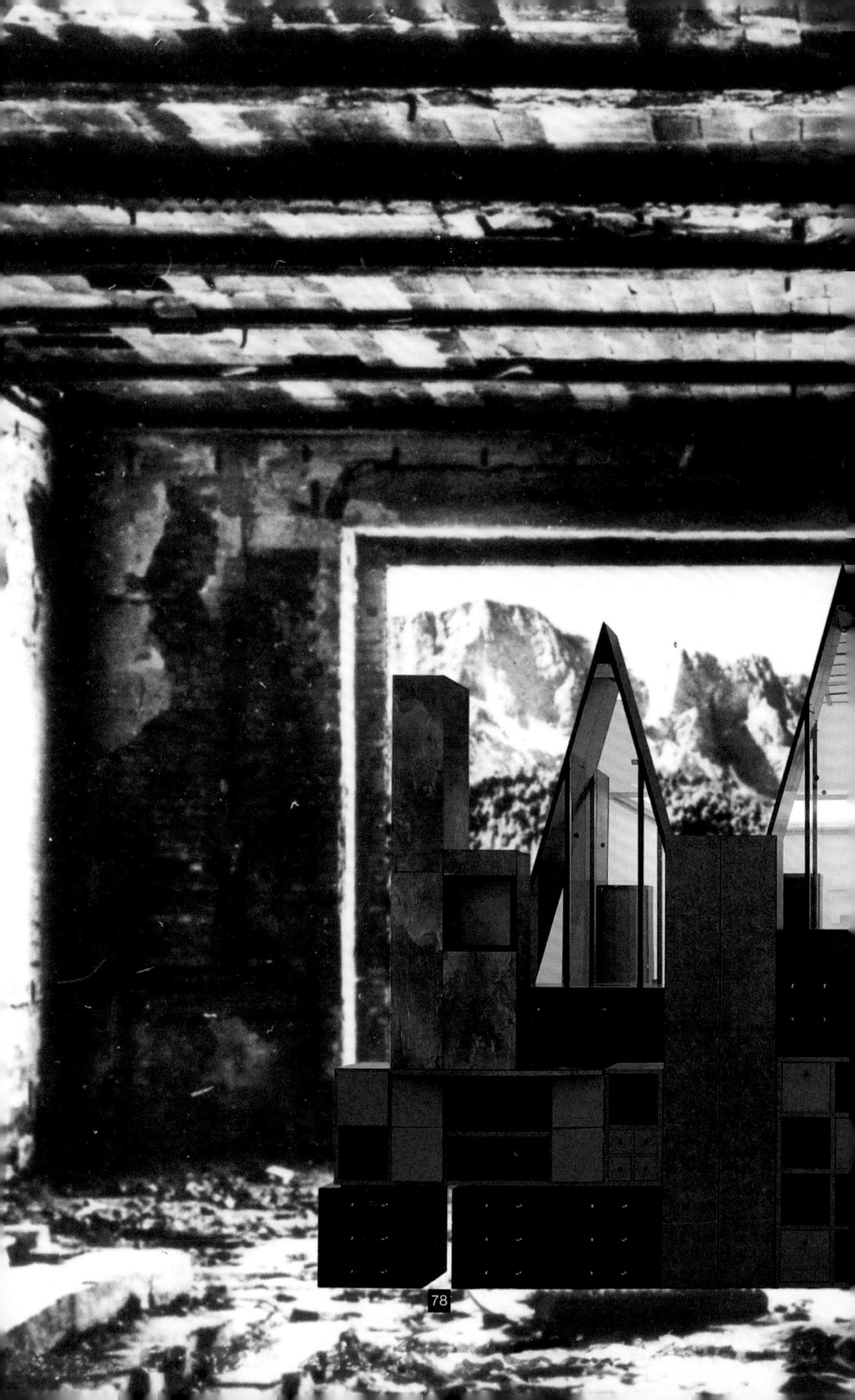

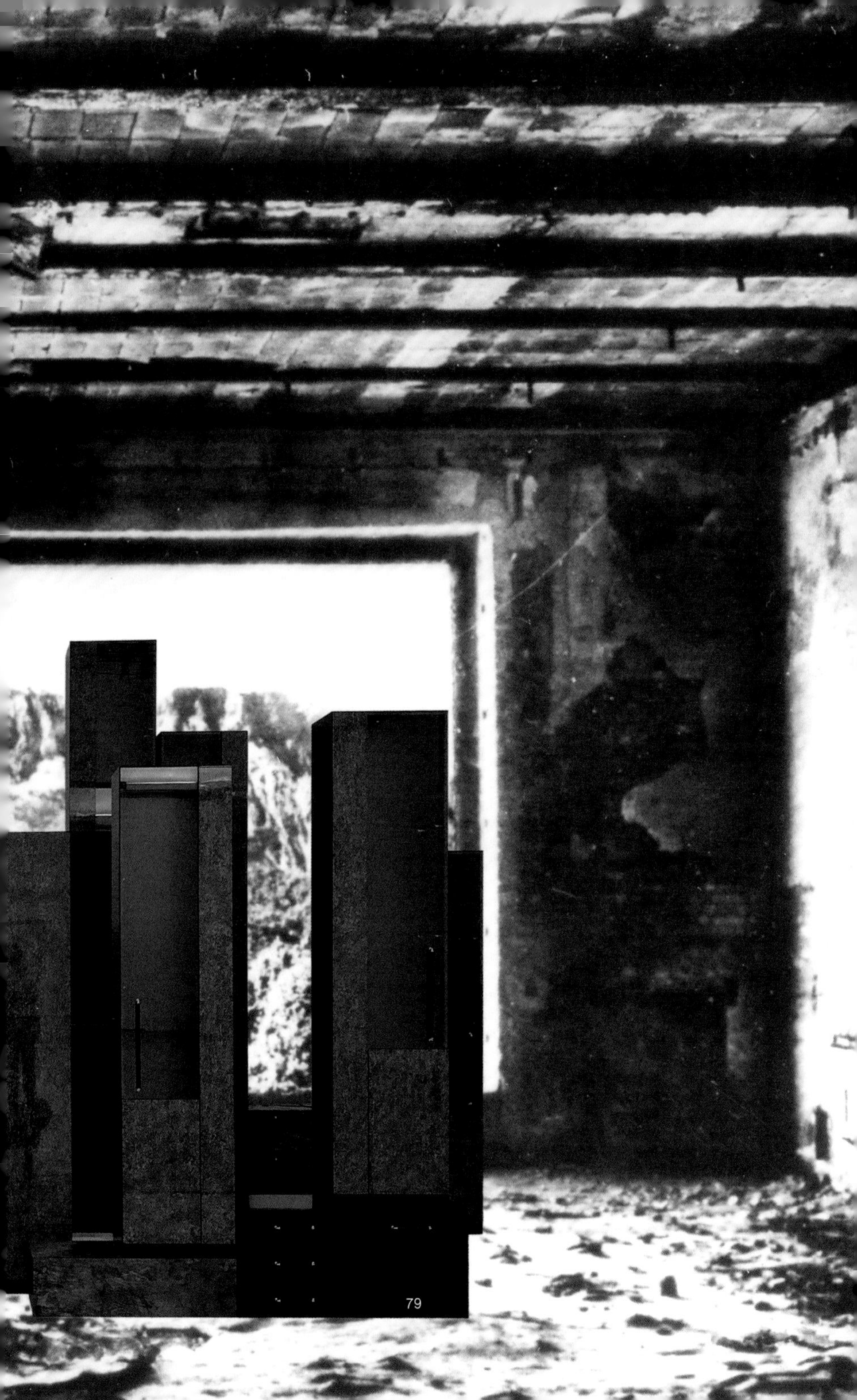

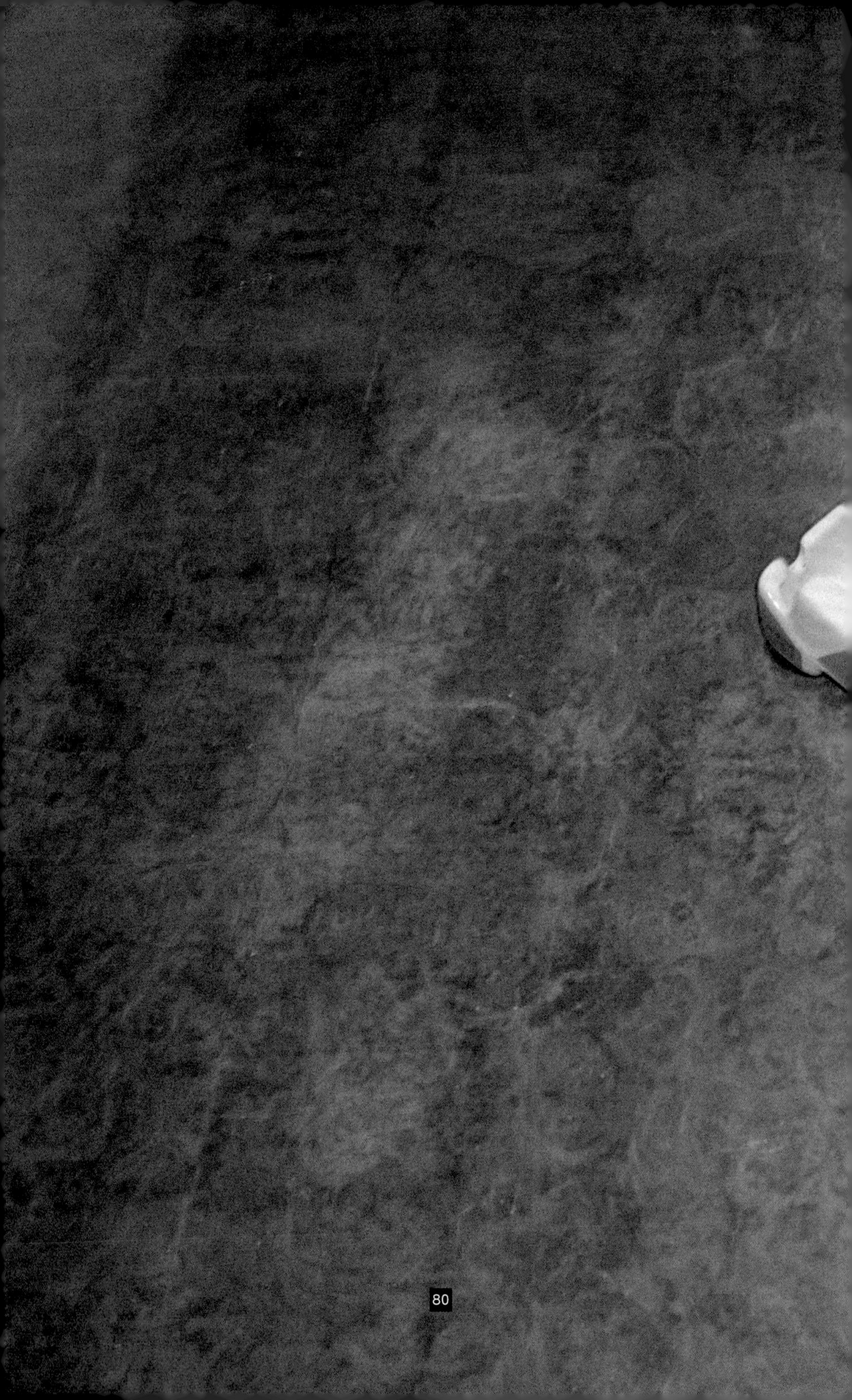

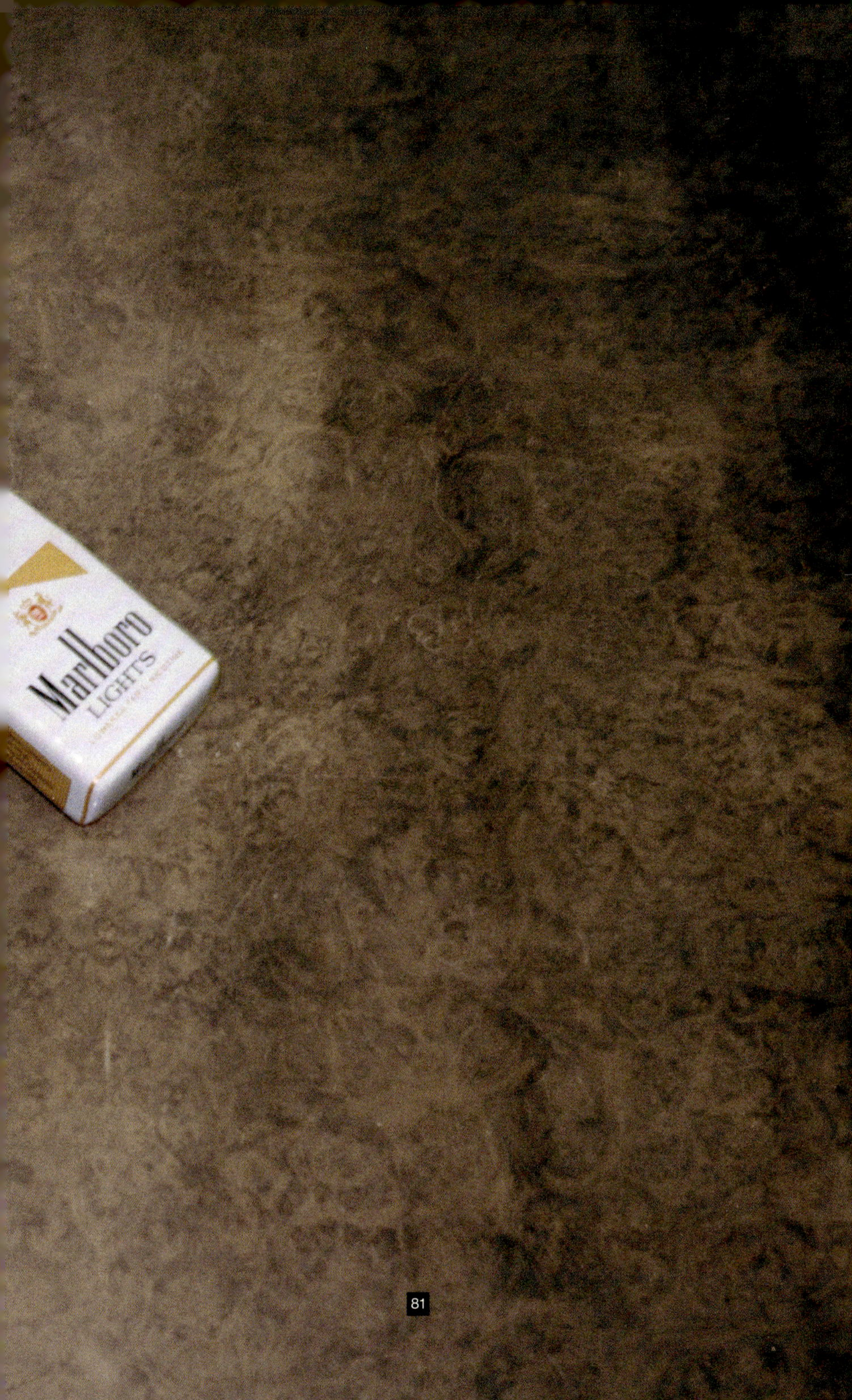
Marlboro
LIGHTS

pp. 42–43
Researching objects and collecting materials at Henrike Naumann's studio, Berlin 2019.

pp. 44–45
In 1937, the Nazis held a festive procession in Munich in celebration of *2000 Years of German Culture* that featured a model of the planned House of German Art.

pp. 46–47
The design drawing from the *2000 Years of German Culture* procession is held in the Haus der Kunst's archive; Henrike Naumann integrated the original into her installation. The framed drawing rests on two club tables from the storeroom of the legendary nightclub P1, located in the same building.

pp. 48–49
In 1957, the Haus der Kunst mounted an exhibition of Emil Nolde's art. As at the inaugural documenta in 1955, the walls were covered with white fabrics. In the exhibition *Degenerate Art* in Munich (1937), the crowded and chaotic hanging was meant to devalue the art on display. Wall hanging *Kandinsky*, eBay Kleinanzeigen, Munich 2019.

pp. 50–51
Ruinenwert, installation view, video *Brecher*, 2019.

pp. 52–53
View of Obersalzberg from the Great Hall of the Berghof, photographed by Hitler's photographer Heinrich Hoffmann, Berchtesgaden 1936.

pp. 54–55
The installation *Ruinenwert* combines furniture from the Haus der Kunst's basement, designed for the erstwhile House of German Art by Atelier Troost, with furniture from eBay Kleinanzeigen, Munich 2019.

pp. 56–57
Draft design with materials samples for the Great Hall of the Berghof from the estate of Gerdy Troost, undated. Wall-to-wall carpet *Toronto Rosa* from Poco Domäne, Munich 2019.

pp. 58–59
Installation *Ruinenwert* as seen when entering the exhibition through the fireplace, Haus der Kunst, Munich 2019.

pp. 60–61
Alpine panorama composed of wall units *Modell Toscana*, eBay Kleinanzeigen, Munich 2019.

pp. 62–63
The Fuhrer's table setting in the „*First German Architecture and Arts and Crafts Exhibition* at the House of German Art, Munich 1938.

pp. 64–65
Ruinenwert, installation view, Haus der Kunst, Munich 2019.

pp. 66–67
Assembly instructions *Modell Toscana*, eBay Kleinanzeigen, Munich 2019.
Merry Christmas postcard *Our Fuhrer's Christmas tree in Berchtesgaden*.

pp. 68–69
Ruinenwert, installation view, Haus der Kunst, Munich 2019.

pp. 70–71
Design drawing for a cabinet, Atelier Troost, from the estate of Gerdy Troost, undated.

pp. 72–77
Ruinenwert, installation views, Haus der Kunst, Munich 2019.

pp. 78–79
Photograph of the destroyed Berghof, Berchtesgaden 1945.

pp. 80–81
Ruinenwert, detail, Haus der Kunst, Munich 2019.

The Ruins of the German Living Room

Henrike Naumann in conversation with Andreas Brandolini

Henrike Naumann As a student, I felt like the division between applied and independent art was unnecessarily rigid. I was born in Zwickau in 1984. I initially studied stage design at the Dresden University of Fine Arts, then scenography at the Babelsberg Film Academy. I've worked as an artist since 2011. Furniture has always been my medium of choice. What I try to do with furniture is not only talk about the design and motivation behind it, but to interpret it beyond that, to add a charge to it, and to ask: can you talk about politics and history through furniture? My work is similar to that of an archaeologist: for me, furniture and objects are documentary forms. In my installations, for example, I thematize the social effects of the postmodern building boom from 1990 onward on the lives of people in the former GDR, or what furniture from the Nazi era does to us when it is placed in a room together with postmodernism's legacies to reveal an anachronistic study and inventory of the past.

With the fall of the Wall, postmodernism—in the form of cheap copies—moved into the new German state's living environments, a theme that I address in many of my installations.. In fact, it was postmodern copies that first prompted me to consider the originals. I started to approach postmodernism almost in reverse, via its legacies.

Andreas Brandolini, you were born in 1951 in the Saxon town of Taucha. You studied architecture in the 1970s at the Technical University of Berlin, which, at that time, was firmly committed to Functionalism. Criticism of (Neo-)Functionalism, which had become Formalism, quickly became a central theme in your work. After two years of practice as a designer and architect at Produktentwicklung Roericht in Ulm, you became self-employed in 1981, accepted a teaching position at the Berlin University of the Arts, founded the project Bellefast—Workshop for Experimental Design in Berlin together with Joachim B. Stanitzek in 1982, and ran Brandolini—Büro für Gestaltung from 1986 to 1993. This was followed by teaching positions at the Hochschule für Gestaltung Offenbach, the Technical University of Graz, the Architectural Association London, the Royal College of Art London, and the University of São Paulo. From 1989 to 2017, you taught as a professor at the Hochschule der Bildenden Künste Saar in Saarbrücken in the product design program, focusing on furniture and interior design.

How would you describe your relationship to the tradition of the Ulm School? Has this relationship changed during your creative practice?

Andreas Brandolini I spent all of my school years in Ulm. When I was young, of course I was aware of what was being done at the Ulm School of Design. This was reinforced by a friend whose parents were very involved in the university. In addition to teaching, his father also ran his own design studio there. That sparked my interest and certainly encouraged me pursue a design profession myself.

Towards the end of my school years, I began to understand what was being taught and done at the university. I understood that it was in the Bauhaus tradition, that the design process—whether it's a house or a lighter—is a rational process of identifying functional and constructive/technical relationships to arrive at a suitable design. This sounded very tempting because it seemed to bring the design process down from the heavens of aesthetic intuition to the earth in terms of what can be done and explained (including to myself). Through abstract exercises in form and composition, the formal repertoire for implementing design ideas developed in the analyses—i.e., in the context of function, handling, and technology—was mapped out. This was the aesthetic foundation. This was accomplished in clear distinction to art, which was frowned upon by most lecturers and students—unless it was "concrete."

During my studies at the Technical University of Berlin, I quickly realized that the framework conditions for architecture were far more complex than I could entirely explain with simple formulas. A significant role was played by the increasingly vocal criticism of the then prevailing urban planning practice of demolishing entire, historically-grown city quarters for new planning and constructing faceless satellite towns on the periphery. This led me to look at old building renovation as an alternative and become more involved with building and urban development history. I became aware of the communicative function of architecture.

Robert Venturi provided sustenance for this with his books *Complexity and Contradiction in Architecture* (1966) and, of course, *Learning from Las Vegas* (1972). These were real taboo breaches that changed common architectural discussions and encouraged me to seek experimental ways of design after graduating. On top of that, in the late 1970s and 1980s, there were radical subcultural movements, especially in music, fashion, and the liberal arts. There was a taboo mood of upheaval—a liberation from post-war and economic miracle culture. I also wanted to contribute, in my own way.

Today, the discourse is even more heterogeneous and diverse. Through postmodernism, the spectrum of functional and aesthetic approaches to design has increased enormously. The rapidly developing digitalization in planning and execution has changed building and product design to an even greater extent. Things are possible today that weren't even conceived of back then, except in movies, books, or science fiction comics. The requirements placed on architecture and design have become much more complex. These can only be answered through the traditional working methods of Functionalism to a limited extent—except in those cases when they are celebrated as a fashionable lifestyle.

However, something that has become an increasingly important topic in the face of advancing globalization is the question of tradition, identity, diversity, and, of course, climate change. I'm following this with great interest, especially considering that some of the answers that have been put forth have become much more subtle and diverse.

HN You are considered one of the founders of the 1980s avant-garde *New German Design.* Your installation *The German Living Room,* shown at documenta 8 in 1987, has received considerable attention. It shows a living room scene: a two-seater couch and two armchairs are placed around a legged, sausage-shaped table, the large campfire rug beneath them adds an element of coziness. Just outside the rug's outline is the so-called *Pony Express,* a television with saddlebags handcrafted from leather on the side. References from different, seemingly distant eras come together to form an anachronistic yet familiar structure. The archaic motif of the campfire was integrated into the middle-class living room and as a news-carrying rider from the Wild West, the television became an almost personal messenger of the digital age.

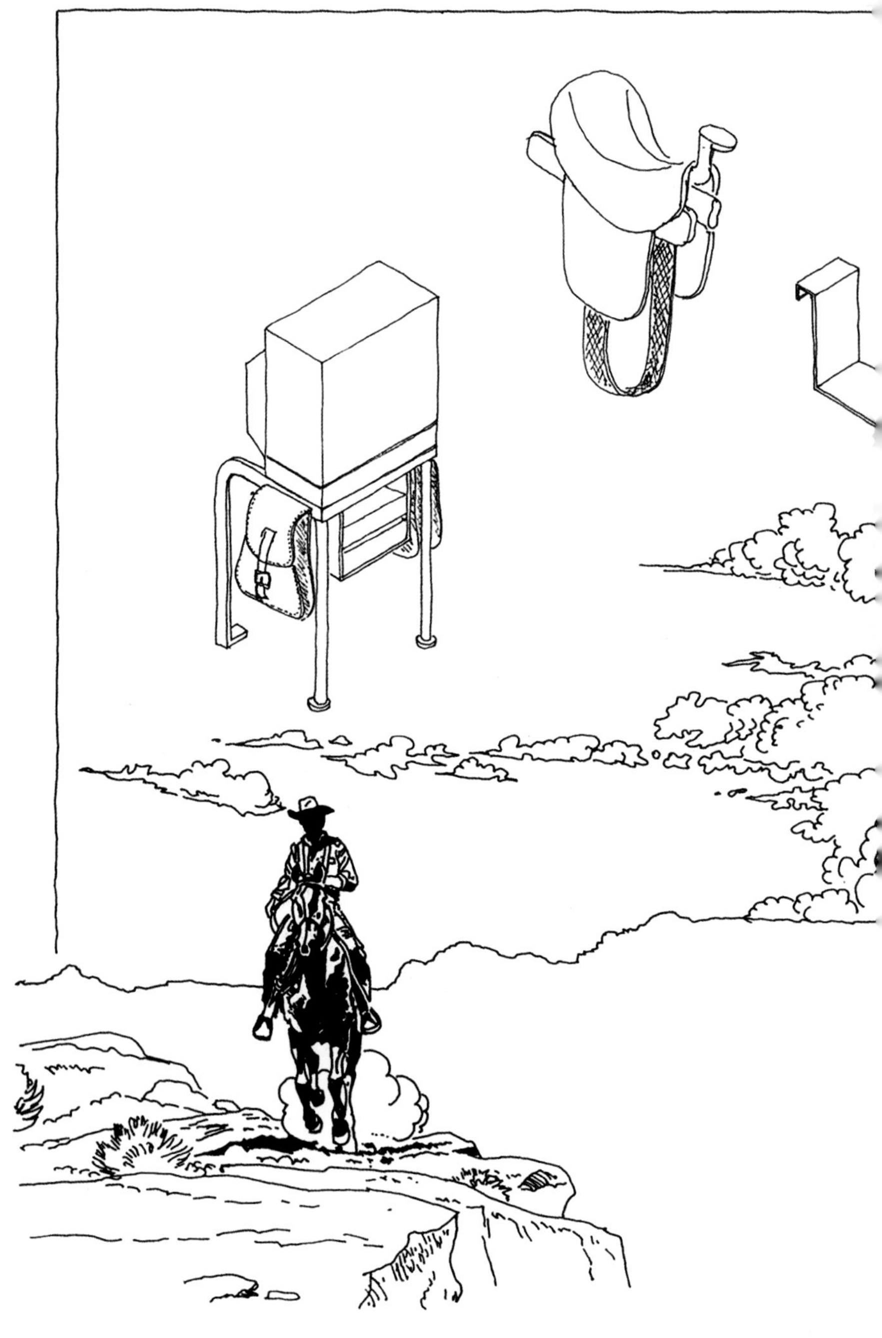

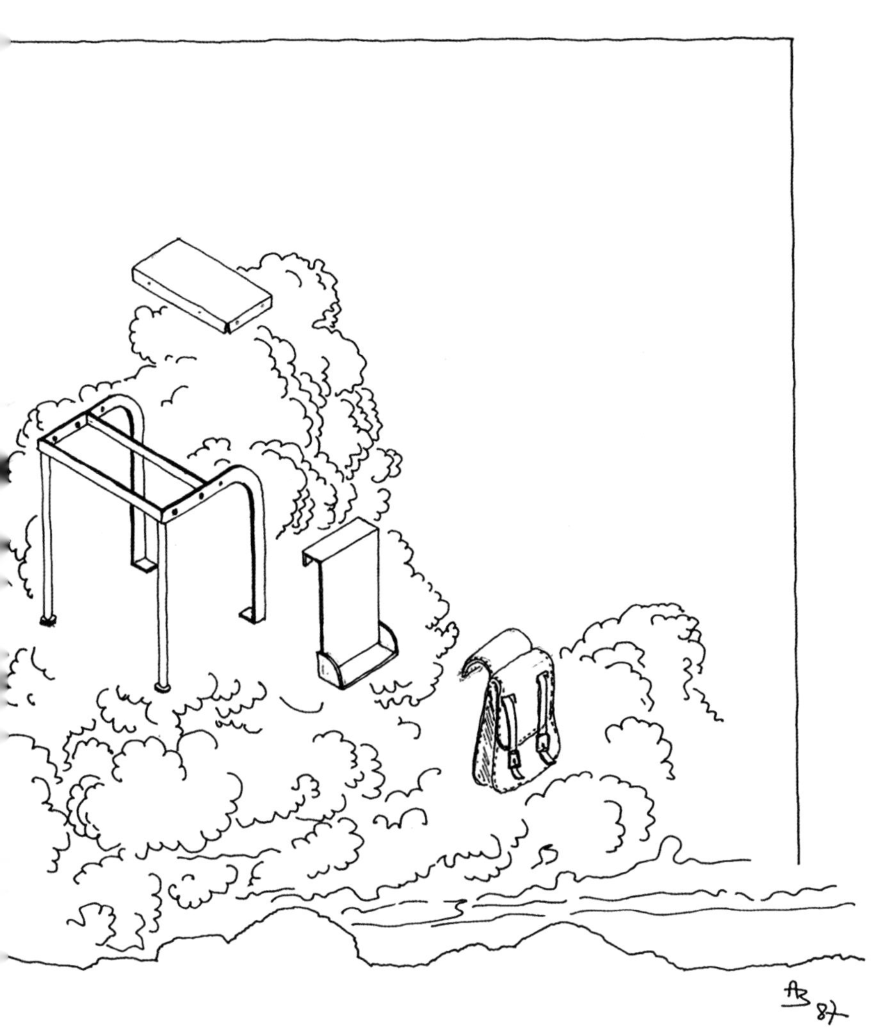

PONY-EXPRESS

Andreas Brandolini, *Pony Express,* drawing, 1987

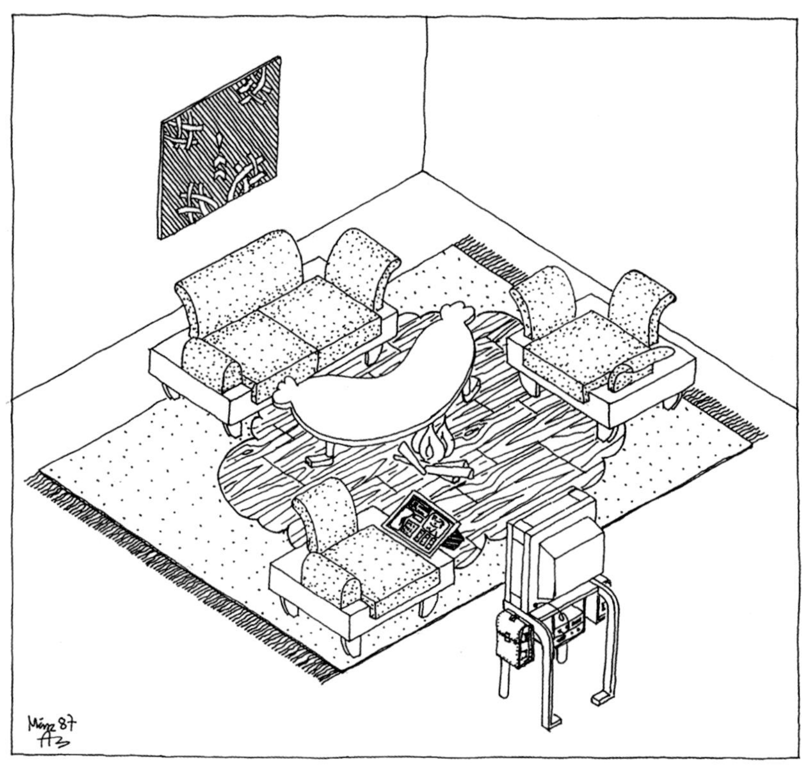

Andreas Brandolini, *The German Living Room,* drawing, 1987

What I think is especially exciting about this work is the interweaving of different levels and epochs, the mix of different signs and cultural references, which consciously illustrate a sense of complexity and inconsistency. In an interview, you said that books about past design epochs always create the impression that everything was homogeneous back then—a gross simplification and reduction. For example, people prefer to talk about the "Nazi style" instead of questioning the origins and continuity of the various, disparate design elements. This would mean a constant uncomfortable process of critical consciousness-raising.

Although your work does not have any direct references to the ruin value theory of the Nazi era as investigated by Angela Schönberger, the critique of dogmas and ideologies that you have formulated and embodied, and your contribution to reducing objects not only to their form and function, but also including the social, political, historical, and technological context, seems quite significant to me.

What's your understanding of the connection between design and politics? Can good design make society better? Has your attitude towards this changed over time?

AB I do believe that a political attitude is reflected in the results of design work. In addition to their functionality, they always answer the question: How do we want to live? That's where I have to position myself as a designer—whether I want to or not.

With the living room, I wanted to demonstrate that our desires and needs are mainly related to what we know: a mix of different, bygone times and what possibilities are or could be available to us today. In the form of the living room, I formulated this as a small three-dimensional and functional story to draw attention to the everyday, modest things and actions. That was also intended to be quite political. The visual language I used was that of comics, which I partially quoted in the drawings.

To claim that the world becomes better through "good design" is, in my opinion, a bit audacious. But you can certainly make it more sustainable, more interesting, and also friendlier. That would be achieving a lot. I also think a little more humor would be a good thing.

When I think about experimental design today, the first thing that comes to mind is digital media, which can be used to check design theses very quickly—both formally and functionally.

The means of production for this are becoming increasingly "democratic," i.e., more readily available. Today work takes place on larger and smaller scales

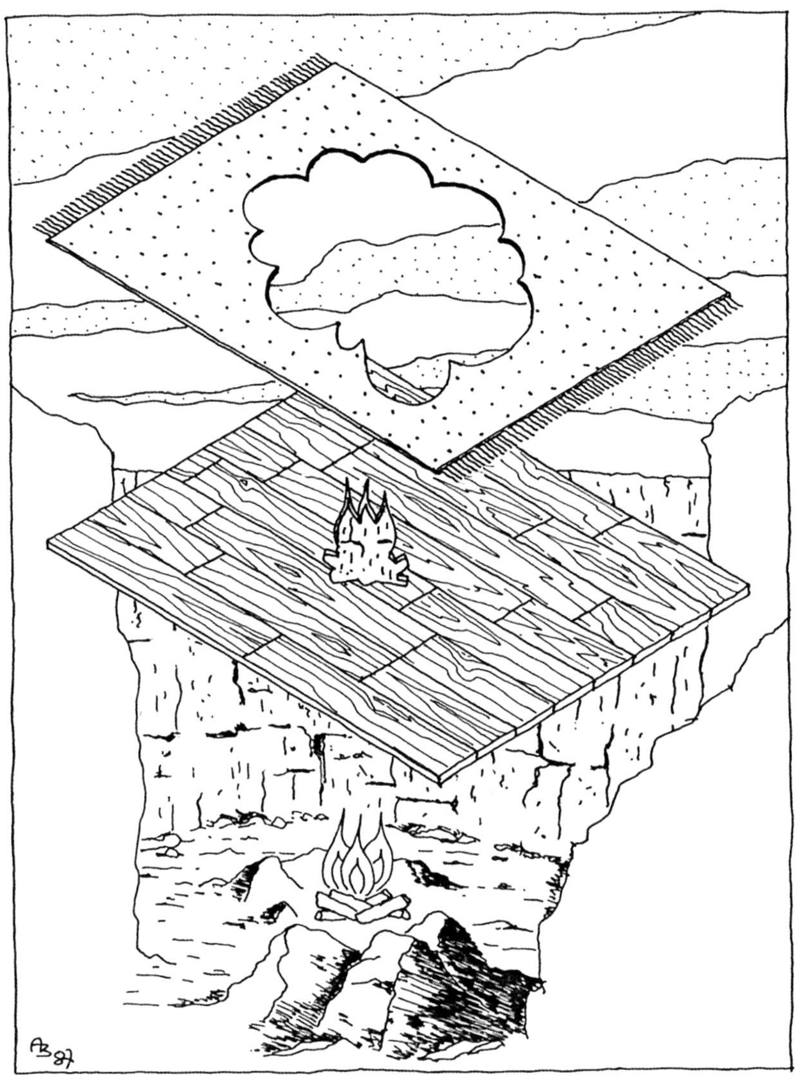

Andreas Brandolini, *The German Living Room,* drawing, 1987

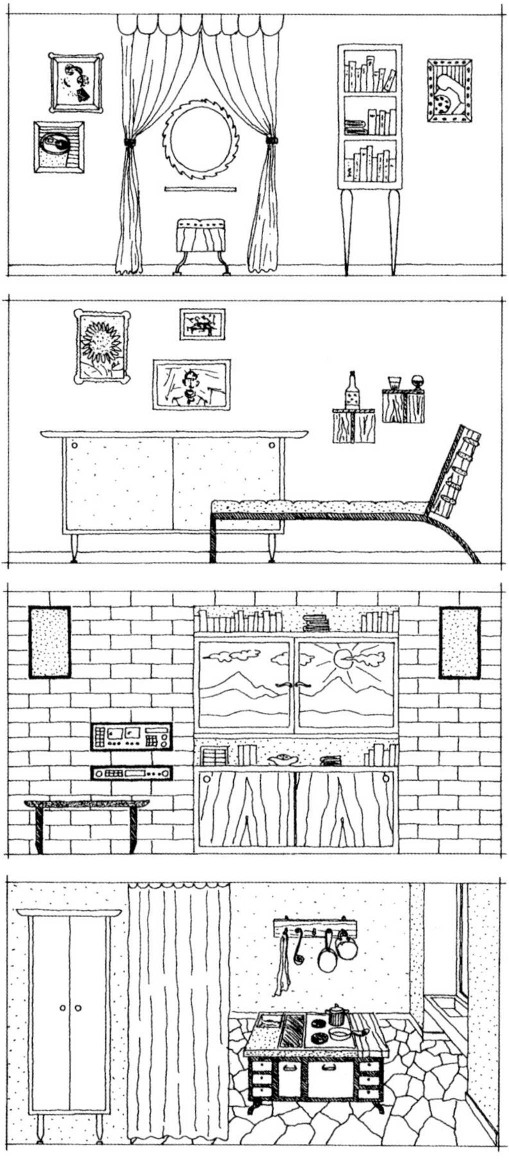

Andreas Brandolini, *Les avant-gardes du mobilier,*
drawings, 1988

for individualized on-demand products or constantly changing small series. This creates new opportunities for economic existence in the face of a globalized economy. This hasn't been utopian for a long time, but is already underway and thus, surprisingly, ties back to the aspirations of the Arts and Crafts movement of the nineteenth century. It propagated a regionally working, artistically-oriented craft.

HN Despite the complexities and the many discontinuities: there is a certain constant, a stability in the way we live in and furnish our surroundings. Your note on *The German Living Room* reads: "Living is conservative. Across all style epochs and trends, the basic elements of bourgeois living have always remained the same. From time to time, a superficial makeover takes place to give the appropriate garb to the belief in progress and in the 'betterment' of ideas. This can be 'futuristic' or 'tradition-conscious' or 'contemporary' or whatever: The foundations of sedentariness remain untouched. But the 'new,' the 'finally good' postulate is always proclaimed with vehemence. What then remains—after years—are things that offer the broadest associative background for looking back on a past epoch—for the historian."

These contradictory demands on designers to "invent something new" and yet only change surfaces without touching the "foundations of sedentariness" are something you repeatedly make the subject of your practice. Are you more interested in working with surfaces and existing concepts than in a symbolic new beginning in design?

AB I didn't want to tear down the "foundations of sedentariness" then or now. I am only interested in finding out how its design changes over time, how social and economic changes affect it. On the surface, these are the first things you perceive. Like people who have changed their outfits and styling. I wonder if that means something or if it's just following a momentary stylistic impulse. But then that would also mean something.

HN There are cross-connections between Angela Schönberger's work and yours. *The German Living Room* was shown a year after documenta 8 at the exhibition *Berlin, Les avant-gardes du mobilier* in Paris, curated by Angela Schönberger as director of Berlin's International Design Center.

In her essay, Angela Schönberger posits that the theory of ruin value was an afterthought and that construction in reinforced concrete was ostensibly rejected for ideological and aesthetic reasons. The massive construction method can be explained primarily by the high iron requirements of the armaments industry.

In a text entitled *Design Poker,* you write: "In the

last twenty years, industrial design has degenerated from an experimental, dynamic profession to a craft dominated—almost exclusively—by production techniques and marketing strategies."

Could a similar conclusion be drawn concerning industrial design? Was and is it more the market that dictates design, and does Functionalism instead serve as legitimation?

AB There is nothing wrong with products that are characterized by high functionality. Advertising them as such is always legitimate. It would be difficult if designers only claimed functionality for themselves and then also used the same repertoire of forms when creating their products. Where would the difference exist that would make us consumers buy one product or the other? I believe that successful products must appeal to many more levels in people than just their need for functionality. Although, I don't want to deny that there are very aesthetic, extremely simple, and rationally designed things or houses whose fascination arises less from their utility value than from their symbolic, sculptural, object-like quality. There simply seems to be "something else" that subtly tempts us to appreciate these things or even to want to own them. Incidentally, Karl Marx wrote about this—from a different perspective—in his reflections on "commodity fetishism." Or Max Weber

Der gestaltete Gegenstand

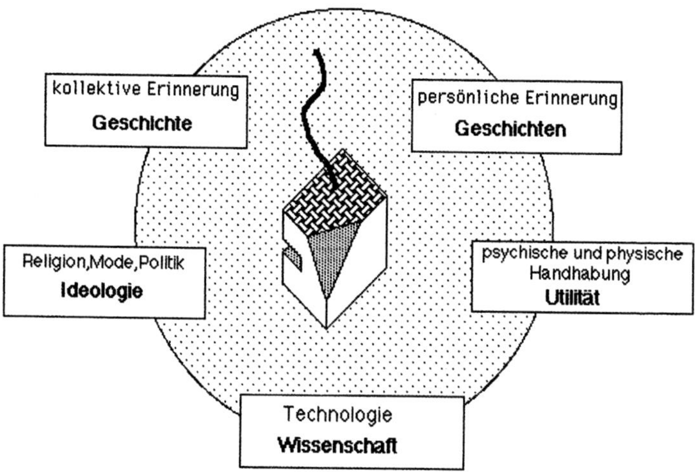

als das Ergebnis einer assoziativen Empirie

Andreas Brandolini, *The Designed Object,* chart, undated

in the treatise *The Protestant Ethic and the Spirit of Capitalism* (1904), which could lead us to see in the motto of functionalism "less is more" a pietistic creed.

HN The graphic *Der gestaltete Gegenstand* (The Designed Object) shows this as a complex, determined by history, ideology, science, handling, and personal memories. In the catalog Berlin: *Les avant-gardes du mobilier,* you say, "Furniture or furnishings have always been an expression of cultural or family identity."

I often question the relationship between collective and personal memory and to what extent associations and feelings that one's own furniture evokes coincide with those of outsiders.

Where would you place the person designing the object in the graphic? Are they an (invisible) part of the graphic, are they looking at the graphic, or are they the table on which the graphic lies?

AB The person designing works on the object in the center of the circle. All around hover forces that influence the design process. There is no rule of thumb for their importance. It must be adjusted constantly. Therefore, the graphic is not an instruction for action. But it can help to situate and understand one's own design activities in a social context. Symbolically, as Freud would have it, the designed object is placed on the table or the chaise longue.

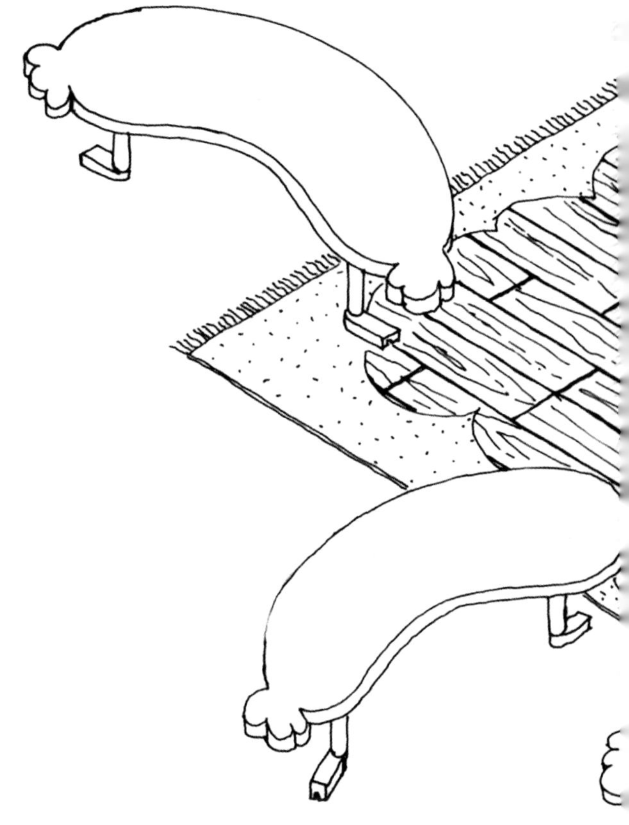

Andreas Brandolini, *The German Living Room,* drawing, 1987

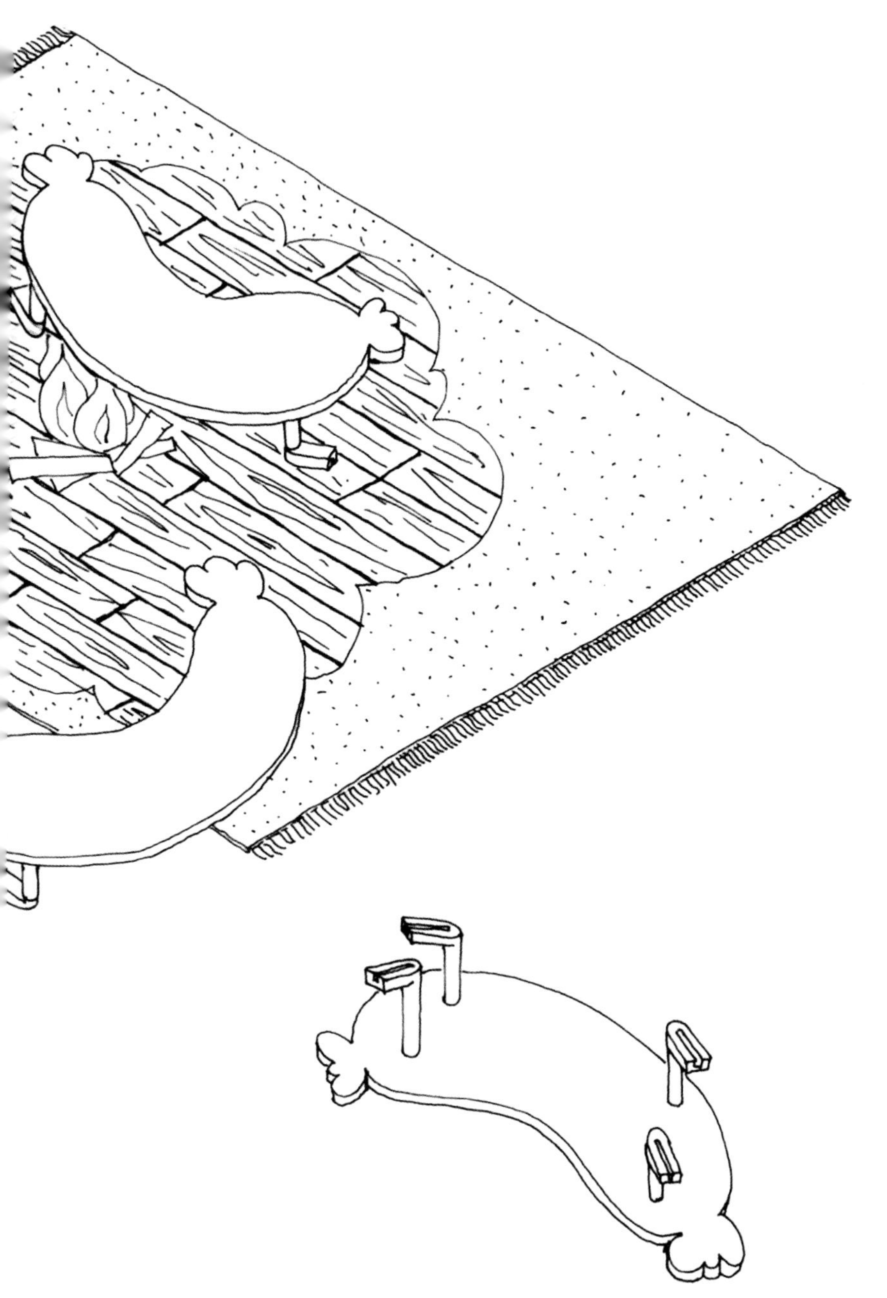

HN In an article by Michael Erlhoff about *The German Living Room,* it says that you would have liked to have explained your installation by saying that you once found a book with drawings by a famous kidney table designer in a ruined building, which in a way brings us to the ruins of postwar Germany and Speer's ruin value theory. Speer dreamt of beautiful ruins. As mighty architectural witnesses of the past, they were intended to convey permanence and timeless validity and to form the bridge of tradition to future generations demanded by Hitler. Schönberger writes that natural stone has always been valued as an expression of aesthetic quality and as cladding for buildings as a "smooth skin." Natural stone was described by Speer as the "most beautiful, natural building material" and thus propagated as the true German building material.

In your practice, you oppose the one, final form and position yourself as being for a playful diversity. Your book *Der Haken* (The Hook) states, "The 'timeless,' 'eternal' design is a product of fear. We proclaim restlessness as the normal state, restlessness as the resting place."

In the end, the "Third Reich's" stony magnificent, representational buildings lay in ruins, no different from the fields of rubble in residential areas.

Was that ruined building, in which you would have liked to have found the book of a famous kidney table designer, a ruin of stone or concrete?

AB It really doesn't matter—the joke only shows that both collective and private memories can be very deceptive and that sometimes desire is father to the memory. With a little bit of detective's intuition, however, it's possible to unmask this.

HN In an article, I read that you personally used *The German Living Room* for a long time. Is that true? Did you live in the installation? If so, why?

AB This wasn't so strange. First, I mostly used furniture design prototypes at home, and I often received "proof copies" of designs as part of commissioned work or from manufacturers. In the case of *The German Living Room,* it was because I moved from Berlin to France and had to give up my storage space. I don't have a winterized storage facility in France, but I do have a large house. So, *The German Living Room* became "my living room" for several years.

List of figures and image credits

p. 14, fig. 1: Albert Speer, extension to the New Reich Chancellery in Berlin, façade on Voßstraße, 1939. Source: Albert Speer Privatarchiv, Heidelberg.

p. 15, fig. 2: Ruins of the New Reich Chancellery, façade on Voßstraße, 1946. Source: unknown.

p. 17, fig. 3: Albert Speer, Zeppelin Field grandstand in Nuremberg, 1938. Source: Werner Rittich, *Architektur und Bauplastik der Gegenwart*, Berlin 1938, p. 24.

p. 18, fig. 4: Antonio Chichi, Amphitheatrum Flavium (Colosseum), Rome, cork model, undated. Source: Hessisches Landesmuseum Kassel.

p. 22, fig. 5: Paul Ludwig Troost, House of German Art, Munich, 1938. Source: Werner Rittich, *Architektur und Bauplastik der Gegenwart*, Berlin 1938, p. 16.

p. 23, fig. 6: Paul Ludwig Troost, NSDAP Fuhrer and Administration Building at Königsplatz in Munich, 1938. Source: Werner Rittich, *Architektur und Bauplastik der Gegenwart*, Berlin 1938 p. 11.

p. 26, fig. 7: Albert Speer, German Pavilion at the World's Fair in Paris, 1937. Source: *Deutschland in Paris. Ein Bild-Buch von Heinrich Hoffmann*, Munich 1937, p. 7.

p. 29, fig. 8: Albert Speer, Model of the Great Hall in Berlin, undated. Source: Albert Speer, *Architektur. Arbeiten 1933–1942*, Berlin/Frankfurt/Vienna 1978, p. 67.

p. 32, fig. 9: The Parthenon, undated. Source: unknown.

p. 33, fig. 10: Iron frame construction, Berlin, undated. Source: Albert Speer, *Stein statt Eisen*, in: *Der Vierjahresplan. Zeitschrift für nationalsozialistischer Wirtschaftspolitik*, 1, 1937, pp. 135ff.

p. 37, fig. 11: Ruin of the New Reich Chancellery, aerial photo, Berlin 1949. Source: unknown.

pp. 44–45: Procession in celebration of *2000 Years of German Culture* featuring a model of the planned House of German Art, Munich, 1937. Source: Zentralinstitut für Kunstgeschichte, Photothek.

pp. 48–49: Exhibition view of Emil Nolde's art at Haus der Kunst, Munich, 1957. Source: Künstlerverbund im Haus der Kunst, Munich.
Exhibition view *Degenerate Art,* Munich, 1937. Source: VG Bild-Kunst, Bonn, bpk/Zentralarchiv, SMB.